CELEBRATING
THE MARIAN YEAR
Devotional Celebrations in Honor of
Mary, Mother of God

(Minister's Edition)

Secretariat
Bishops' Committee on the Liturgy
National Conference of Catholic Bishops

In its planning document, as approved by the general membership of the National Conference of Catholic Bishops in November 1986, the Secretariat of the Bishops' Committee on the Liturgy was authorized to prepare devotional Marian resources. *Celebrating the Marian Year* (Minister's Edition) was approved for publication by the members of the Bishops' Committee on the Liturgy on March 23, 1987, and is authorized for publication by the undersigned.

Monsignor Daniel F. Hoye
General Secretary
NCCB/USCC

April 1, 1987

Contents

Introduction

In his apostolic exhortation *Marialis cultus* Pope Paul VI stated that "even as she is the model of the Church as a whole in its worship of God, Mary is clearly also the *teacher of devotion* for individual Christians" (no. 21). For, the Blessed Virgin magnified and praised the Lord for the great things God accomplished in her, his lowly servant. As St. Ambrose says, "May the mind of Mary be in all to magnify the Lord; her spirit, to rejoice in God."

The Mother of God stands at the center of the Church's devotional life, both as the teacher and object of devotion. This was clearly reaffirmed by of the Second Vatican Council in the "Dogmatic Constitution on the Church," *Lumen Gentium:* "Mary, as the Mother of God, placed by grace next to her Son above all angels and saints, has shared in the mysteries of Christ and is justly honored by a special veneration in the Church" (no. 66). Especially from the time of the Council of Ephesus (431), when the Church affirmed that Mary is the Mother of God, *Theotokos* ("God-bearer"), devotion to Mary increased "in veneration and love, in invocation and imitation, according to her own prophetic words: 'All generations shall call me blessed, because he that is mighty hath done great things for me' (Lk 1:48-49)" (ibid.).

The Council taught that devotion to the Mother of God

as it has always existed in the Church, even though it is altogether special, is essentially distinct from the worship of adoration paid equally to the Word incarnate, the Father, and the Holy Spirit. Honoring Mary contributes to that adoration. For the various forms of Marian devotion, sanctioned by the Church within the limits of sound orthodoxy and suited to circumstances of time and place as well as to the character and culture of peoples, have the effect that as we honor the Mother, we also truly know the Son and give love, glory, and obedience to him, through whom all things have their being (see Col 1:15-16) and, "in whom it has pleased the eternal Father that all fullness should dwell (Col 1:19)" (ibid.).

The Second Vatican Council expressly professed the Church's teaching on Mary and counseled "all the Church's children to foster wholeheartedly the cultus—especially the liturgical cultus—of the Blessed Virgin" (ibid., no. 67). And, in response to that conciliar teaching, Pope Paul VI, in the apostolic exhortation *Marialis cultus* (February 2, 1974), specifi-

1

cally called for the renewal of devotions to the Virgin Mary:

> . . . the faithful's devotion and acts of veneration toward the Mother of God have also taken different forms, corresponding to historical and local circumstances and varying attitudes and cultures of peoples. One result is that the forms expressing devotion and subject to the conditions of the times seem in need of a reform that will eliminate the ephemeral, retain what is of enduring value, and integrate those truths of faith that have been reached from theological investigation and affirmed by the Church's magisterium (no. 24).

Pope Paul VI invited bishops and others to revise the form and practice of devotion toward the Virgin Mary, provided that "there be respect for tradition and openness to the legitimate demands of our contemporaries" (ibid.). Marian devotions, accordingly, must be revised to "clearly evidence their intrinsically Trinitarian and Christological character" (ibid.). In addition, they must manifest "the Person and action of the Holy Spirit" (ibid.).

This collection of Marian devotions is an attempt to respond to both the Council's teaching on Marian devotion and that of Pope Paul VI in *Marialis cultus*. In the context of that teaching, Pope John Paul II, on the solemnity of Mary, Mother of God (January 1, 1987), proclaimed a Marian Year to commence on Pentecost, June 7, 1987, and to conclude on the solemnity of the Assumption, August 15, 1988. The purpose of the

Marian Year is stated by Pope John Paul II in the encyclical *Redemptoris Mater* (March 25, 1987):

> . . . the Marian Year is meant to promote a new and more careful reading of what the Council said about the Blessed Virgin Mary, Mother of God, in the mystery of Christ and of the Church, the topic to which the contents of this Encyclical are devoted. Here we speak not only of *the doctrine of faith* but also of *the life of faith,* and thus of authentic "Marian spirituality," seen in the light of Tradition, and especially the spirituality to which the Council exhorts us. Furthermore, Marian *spirituality,* like its corresponding *devotion,* finds a very rich source in the historical experience of individuals and of the various Christian communities present among the different peoples and nations of the world . . . (no. 48).

The Church's tradition of honoring the Mother of God has found expression in a number of solemnities and feasts linked to the paschal mystery of Jesus Christ. Likewise, through the centuries, various forms of popular devotion and piety have arisen that have their source both in the liturgy and in Marian spirituality.

The devotional services in this collection take their inspiration from both the liturgy and from that spirituality to which *Redemptoris Mater* alludes. They provide forms for public devotion to the Mother of God that are both theologically and liturgically sound and also respect the traditions of Marian devotion to which we are heirs. The celebrations may be led by a priest, deacon, or lay person.

In addition to the services, official liturgical texts and contemporary translations of traditional devotional prayers have been included in order that these services might be in harmony with the revised liturgical books.

Thus, the affirmation of the bishops of the United States of America, in their pastoral letter of 1973 *Behold Your Mother: Woman of Faith*, has taken concrete form:

We Bishops of the United States wish to affirm with all our strength the lucid statements of the Second Vatican Council on the permanent importance of authentic devotion to the Blessed Virgin, not only in the liturgy, where the Church accords her a most special place under Jesus her Son, but also in the beloved devotions that have been repeatedly approved and encouraged by the Church and that are still filled with meaning for Catholics (no. 93).

The celebration of the Marian Year, promulgated by Pope John Paul II, provides a fitting occasion for the publication of these devotional services which, it is hoped, will find a suitable place in the prayer life of American Catholics.

Reverend John A. Gurrieri
Executive Director
Secretariat
Bishops' Committee on the Liturgy

Celebration of the Litany of Loreto

Introduction

1. This service is centered around the Litany of Loreto, a Marian litany containing invocations that date back to the twelfth century. It was recorded in its present form (apart from a few additions by recent popes) at Loreto in 1558 and approved by Sixtus V (1521-1590). For about half of the invocations, the present translation uses the traditional renderings, which have been in use since the seventeenth century.

2. The service may be led by a priest, deacon, or lay person.

3. The litany may be led by the minister or by one or more cantors. If it is not possible to sing the litany, instrumental music may be played while the litany is being recited.

4. Appropriate Marian hymns may be sung at the points indicated in the service (see no. 117 below).

5. If desired, a psalm, a hymn, or instrumental music may follow the reading from *Lumen Gentium*.

Celebration of the Litany of Loreto

6. When all have gathered, a suitable song may be sung. The minister makes the sign of the cross, saying:

In the name of the Father, and of the Son, and of the Holy Spirit.

All respond:

Amen.

GREETING

7. The minister greets those present in the following or other suitable words, taken mainly from sacred Scripture:

Praise be to God, who sent us his Son, born of the Virgin Mary. Blessed be God for ever.

All respond:

Blessed be God for ever.

INTRODUCTION

8. The minister introduces the celebration in these or similar words:

We gather today in faith to praise almighty God, who wishes that Mary, the mother of his only-begotten Son, be honored by every generation. We gather to glorify Christ our Savior, who chose the Virgin Mary for his mother. We gather to exalt the Holy Spirit, by whose power Christ was conceived in the womb of Mary. We gather to honor Mary, the holy Mother of God.

OPENING PRAYER

9. The minister says the opening prayer. Additional prayers are given in no. 111.

Let us pray.

10. After a brief period of silent prayer, the minister continues:

Gracious God,
in your wisdom you chose the Virgin Mary from all women
to be the mother of your Son.
She grew in the beauty of grace to be the mystical rose
who offered herself as the dwelling place of the Savior.
Grant that we too may be open to your call
and lead lives of holiness,
so that your word may take flesh within our hearts.

We ask this through Christ our Lord.

> All respond:

Amen.

READING FROM THE WORD OF GOD

> 11. All sit, and a reader then proclaims the first reading from sacred Scripture. Additional readings are given in no. 115.

> 1 Chronicles 15:3-4,15-16;16:1-2
> They brought the ark of God in and put it inside the tent David had pitched for it.

A reading from the first book of Chronicles.

David assembled all Israel in Jerusalem to bring the ark of the Lord to the place which he had prepared for it. David also called together the sons of Aaron and the Levites. The Levites bore the ark of God on their shoulders with poles, as Moses had ordained according to the Word of the Lord.

David commanded the chiefs of the Levites to appoint their brethren as chanters, to play on musical instruments, harps, lyres, and cymbals to make a loud sound of rejoicing.

They brought in the ark of God and set it within the tent which David had pitched for it. Then they offered up holocausts and peace offerings to God. When David had finished offering up the holocausts and peace offerings, he blessed the people in the name of the Lord.

This is the Word of the Lord.

RESPONSE

> 12. As circumstances suggest, the following response or some other suitable song may be sung:

Judith 13:18,19,20

R. You are the highest honor of our race.

Blessed are you, daughter, by the Most High God, above all the women on earth; and blessed be the Lord God, the creator of heaven and earth. R.

Your deed of hope will never be forgotten by those who tell of the might of God. R.

May God make this redound to your everlasting honor, rewarding you with blessings, because you risked your life when your people were being oppressed, and you averted our disaster, walking uprightly before our God. And all the people answered, "Amen! Amen!" R.

GOSPEL

13. The deacon (or, in his absence, the minister) proclaims the gospel:

Matthew 1:1-16,18-23 *(Long Form)* OR Matthew 1:18-23 *(Short Form)*
She has conceived and what is in her is by the Holy Spirit.

(Long Form)

A reading from the holy gospel according to Matthew.

A family record of Jesus Christ, son of David,
son of Abraham. Abraham was the father of
Isaac, Isaac the father of Jacob, Jacob the
father of Judah and his brothers.
Judah was the father of Perez and Zerah,
    whose mother was Tamar.
Perez was the father of Hezron,
Hezron the father of Ram.
Ram was the father of Amminadab,
Amminadab the father of Nahshon,
Nahshon the father of Salmon.
Salmon was the father of Boaz, whose mother
    was Rahab,
Boaz was the father of Obed, whose mother
    was Ruth.
Obed was the father of Jesse,
Jesse the father of King David.
David was the father of Solomon, whose
    mother had been the wife of Uriah.

Solomon was the father of Rehoboam,
Rehoboam the father of Abijah,
Abijah the father of Asa.
Asa was the father of Jehoshaphat,
Jehoshaphat the father of Joram,
Joram the father of Uzziah.
Uzziah was the father of Jotham,
Jotham the father of Ahaz,
Ahaz the father of Hezekiah.
Hezekiah was the father of Manasseh,
Manasseh the father of Amos,
Amos the father of Josiah.
Josiah became the father of Jechoniah and his
    brothers at the time of the Babylonian exile.
After the Babylonian exile
Jechoniah was the father of Shealtiel,
Shealtiel the father of Zerubbabel.
Zerubbabel was the father of Abiud,
Abiud the father of Eliakim,
Eliakim the father of Azor.
Azor was the father of Zadok,
Zadok the father of Achim,
Achim the father of Eliud.
Eliud was the father of Eleazar,
Eleazar the father of Matthan,
Matthan the father of Jacob.
Jacob was the father of Joseph the husband
    of Mary.
It was of her that Jesus who is called the
    Messiah was born.

Now this is how the birth of Jesus Christ came about. When his mother Mary was engaged to Joseph, but before they lived together, she was found with child through the power of the Holy Spirit. Joseph her husband, an upright man unwilling to expose her to the law, decided to divorce her quietly. Such was his intention when suddenly the angel of the Lord appeared in a dream and said to him: "Joseph, son of David, have no fear about taking Mary as your wife. It is by the Holy Spirit that she has conceived this child. She is to have a son and you are to name him Jesus because he will save his people from their sins." All this happened to fulfill what the Lord had said through the prophet:

> "The virgin shall be with child
> and give birth to a son,

and they shall call him Emmanuel,"
a name which means "God is with us."

This is the gospel of the Lord.

OR

(Short Form)

A reading from the holy gospel according to Matthew.

Now this is how the birth of Jesus Christ came about. When his mother Mary was engaged to Joseph, but before they lived together, she was found with child through the power of the Holy Spirit. Joseph her husband, an upright man unwilling to expose her to the law, decided to divorce her quietly. Such was his intention when suddenly the angel of the Lord appeared in a dream and said to him: "Joseph, son of David, have no fear about taking Mary as your wife. It is by the Holy Spirit that she has conceived this child. She is to have a son and you are to name him Jesus because he will save his people from their sins." All this happened to fulfill what the Lord had said through the prophet:

> "The virgin shall be with child
> and give birth to a son,
> and they shall call him Emmanuel,"
> a name which means "God is with us."

This is the gospel of the Lord.

As circumstances suggest, the reading may be followed by a suitable song or instrumental music.

HOMILY

14. The minister may then give those present a brief explanation of the Scripture readings and the role of Mary in God's plan of salvation, or one of the non-biblical readings in no. 116 may be read.

LITANY OF LORETO

15. The litany is then sung or recited. All kneel during the litany, except on Sundays and during the Easter season when they stand.

Lord, have mercy	Lord, have mercy
Christ, have mercy	Christ, have mercy
Lord, have mercy	Lord, have mercy

God our Father in heaven	have mercy on us
God the Son, Redeemer of the world	have mercy on us
God the Holy Spirit	have mercy on us
Holy Trinity, one God	have mercy on us
Holy Mary	pray for us
Holy Mother of God	pray for us
Most honored of virgins	pray for us
Mother of Christ	pray for us
Mother of the Church	pray for us
Mother of divine grace	pray for us
Mother most pure	pray for us
Mother of chaste love	pray for us
Mother and virgin	pray for us
Sinless Mother	pray for us
Dearest of mothers	pray for us
Model of motherhood	pray for us
Mother of good counsel	pray for us
Mother of our Creator	pray for us
Mother of our Savior	pray for us
Virgin most wise	pray for us
Virgin rightly praised	pray for us
Virgin rightly renowned	pray for us
Virgin most powerful	pray for us
Virgin gentle in mercy	pray for us
Faithful Virgin	pray for us
Mirror of justice	pray for us
Throne of wisdom	pray for us
Cause of our joy	pray for us
Shrine of the Spirit	pray for us
Glory of Israel	pray for us
Vessel of selfless devotion	pray for us
Mystical Rose	pray for us
Tower of David	pray for us
Tower of ivory	pray for us
House of gold	pray for us
Ark of the covenant	pray for us
Gate of heaven	pray for us
Morning Star	pray for us
Health of the sick	pray for us
Refuge of sinners	pray for us
Comfort of the troubled	pray for us

Help of Christians	pray for us
Queen of angels	pray for us
Queen of patriarchs and prophets	pray for us
Queen of apostles and martyrs	pray for us
Queen of confessors and virgins	pray for us
Queen of all saints	pray for us
Queen conceived without original sin	pray for us
Queen assumed into heaven	pray for us
Queen of the rosary	pray for us
Queen of peace	pray for us

Lamb of God, you take away the sins of the world	have mercy on us
Lamb of God, you take away the sins of the world	have mercy on us
Lamb of God, you take away the sins of the world	have mercy on us

The minister then says:

Pray for us, holy Mother of God.

And all respond:

That we may become worthy of the promises of Christ.

The minister invites the people to pray:

Let us pray.

After a brief pause for silent prayer, the minister continues:

Eternal God,
let your people enjoy constant health in mind and body.
Through the intercession of the Virgin Mary
free us from the sorrows of this life
and lead us to happiness in the life to come.

Grant this through Christ our Lord.

All respond:

Amen.

PRAYER TO SAINT JOSEPH

16. If desired, the minister may add the following prayer to Saint Joseph, husband of Mary:

Blessed Joseph, husband of Mary, be with us this day.

You protected and cherished the Virgin;
loving the Child Jesus as your Son,
you rescued him from danger of death.
Defend the Church, the household of God,
purchased by the blood of Christ.

Guardian of the holy family,
be with us in our trials.
May your prayers obtain for us
the strength to flee from error
and wrestle with the powers of corruption
so that in life we may grow in holiness
and in death rejoice in the crown of victory.

All respond:

Amen.

At the conclusion of the prayers, all stand.

BLESSING AND DISMISSAL

17. If a priest or deacon presides, he dismisses the people in these or similar words:

Born of the Blessed Virgin Mary, the Son of God redeemed humanity. May he enrich you with his blessings.

All respond:

Amen.

He then adds:

May almighty God bless you, the Father, and the Son, + and the Holy Spirit.

All respond:

Amen.

Deacon (priest):

Let us go in the peace of Christ.

All respond:

Thanks be to God.

A lay minister concludes with the following:

Born of the Blessed Virgin Mary, the Son of God redeemed humanity. May he enrich us always with his blessings.

All respond:

Amen.

---

18. The celebration should end with a song.

Celebration of Petition and Invocation for Mary's Intercession

Introduction

19. It is an ancient tradition to pray to the Blessed Virgin Mary for her intercession that Christians "might receive from the Holy Spirit the power to beget Christ in their own souls" (*Marialis cultus*, no. 26).

20. This service centers around prayer and petition through the intercession of the Blessed Virgin Mary. The celebration may be led by a priest, deacon, or lay person.

21. Two forms of intercession are provided, one taken from the *Liturgy of the Hours* and the other based on the "Akathist Hymn" of the Byzantine liturgy.

22. Appropriate hymns (see no. 117 below) should be chosen for the various parts of the rite, and every effort should be made to ensure full congregational participation.

Celebration of Petition and Invocation for Mary's Intercession

23. When all have gathered, a suitable song may be sung. The minister makes the sign of the cross, saying:

In the name of the Father, and of the Son, and of the Holy Spirit.

All respond:

Amen.

ACCLAMATION OF PRAISE

24. The minister says:

You have been blessed, O Virgin Mary, above all other women on earth by the Lord, the Most High God.

All respond:

He has exalted your name
that your praises shall never fade
from the mouths of God's people.

READING FROM THE WORD OF GOD

25. All sit. The minister says:

Let us be attentive to the Word of God as we hear of Mary's role in God's plan for our salvation.

26. A reader proclaims a text of sacred Scripture. Additional readings are given in no. 115.

Proverbs 8:22-31
Mary, Seat of Wisdom.

A reading from the book of Proverbs.

[Thus speaks the Wisdom of God:]
"The Lord begot me, the firstborn of his ways,
    the forerunner of his prodigies of long ago;
From of old I was poured forth,
    at the first, before the earth.
When there were no depths I was brought forth,
    when there were no fountains of springs of water;
Before the mountains were settled into place,
    before the hills, I was brought forth;
While as yet the earth and the fields were not made,
    nor the first clods of the world.
"When he established the heavens I was there,
    when he marked out the vault over the face of the deep;
When he made firm the skies above,
    when he fixed fast the foundations of the earth;
When he set for the sea its limit,
    so that the waters should not transgress his command;
Then was I beside him as his craftsman,
    and I was his delight day by day,
Playing before him all the while,
    playing on the surface of his earth;
    [and I found delight in the sons of men.]"

This is the Word of the Lord.

OR

During the Easter Season

Acts 1:12-14
They all joined in continuous prayer together with Jesus' mother, Mary.

A reading from the Acts of the Apostles.

[After Jesus had ascended to heaven,] the apostles returned to Jerusalem from the mount called Olive near Jerusalem—a mere sabbath's journey away. Entering the city, they went to the upstairs room where they were staying: Peter and Thomas, Bartholomew and Matthew; James son of Alpheus; Simon, the Zealot party member, and Judas son of James. Together they devoted themselves to constant prayer. There were some women in their company, and Mary the mother of Jesus, and his brothers.

This is the Word of the Lord.

PSALM

27. As circumstances suggest, the following responsorial psalm or some other suitable song may be sung:

Luke 1:46-55

R. The Almighty has done great things for me and holy is his name.

Mary said:
"My being proclaims the greatness of the Lord,
   my spirit finds joy in God my savior. R.

For he has looked upon his servant in her lowliness;
   all ages to come shall call me blessed.
God who is mighty has done great things for me,
   holy is his name. R.

His mercy is from age to age on those who fear him.
He has shown might with his arm;
   he has confused the proud in their inmost thoughts. R.

He has deposed the mighty from their thrones
   and raised the lowly to high places.
The hungry he has given every good thing,
   while the rich he has sent empty away. R.

He has upheld Israel his servant,
   ever mindful of his mercy;
Even as he promised our fathers,
   promised Abraham and his descendants forever." R.

OR

Judith 13:18,19,20.

R. You are the highest honor of our race.

Blessed are you, daughter, by the Most High God, above all the women on earth; and blessed be the Lord God, the creator of heaven and earth. R.

Your deed of hope will never be forgotten by those who tell of the might of God. R.

May God make this redound to your everlasting honor, rewarding you with blessings, because you risked your life when your people were being oppressed, and you averted our disaster, walking uprightly before our God. And all the people answered, "Amen! Amen!" R.

GOSPEL

28. The deacon (or, in his absence, the minister) proclaims the gospel. Additional readings are given in no. 115. All stand.

John 2:1-11
The mother of Jesus was at the wedding feast with him.

A reading from the holy gospel according to John.

There was a wedding at Cana in Galilee, and the mother of Jesus was there. Jesus and his disciples had likewise been invited to the celebration. At a certain point the wine ran out, and Jesus' mother told him, "They have no more wine." Jesus replied, "Woman, how does this concern of yours involve me? My hour has not yet come." His mother instructed those waiting on table, "Do whatever he tells you." As prescribed for Jewish ceremonial washings, there were at hand six stone water jars, each one holding fifteen to twenty-five gallons. "Fill those jars with water," Jesus ordered, at which they filled them to the brim. "Now," he said, "draw some out and take it to the waiter in charge." They did as he instructed them. The waiter in charge tasted the water made wine, without knowing where it had come from; only the waiters knew, since they had drawn the water. Then the waiter in charge called the groom over and remarked to him: "People usually serve the choice wine first; then when the guests have been drinking a while, a lesser vintage. What you have done is keep the choice wine until now." Jesus performed this first of his signs at Cana in Galilee. Thus did he reveal his glory, and his disciples believed in him.

This is the gospel of the Lord.

At the end of the gospel all sit for the homily.

HOMILY

29. The minister may give those present a brief explanation of the Scripture readings and the role of Mary in God's plan of salvation, or one of the non-biblical readings in no. 116 may be read.

30. The homily may be followed by a period of silent reflection, a song, or instrumental music.

INTERCESSIONS

31. The intercessions then follow; one of the following forms is chosen. During the intercessions, all stand.

A. From the *Liturgy of the Hours:*

The minister introduces the intercessions. Another person proclaims the individual intentions. Other intentions appropriate to the occasion may be added.

Let us praise God our almighty Father, who wished that Mary, his Son's mother, be celebrated by each generation. Now in need we ask:

R. Mary, full of grace, intercede for us.

1. You made Mary the mother of mercy,
   may all who are faced with trials feel her motherly love. R.

2. You wished Mary to be the mother of the family in the home of Jesus and Joseph,
   may all mothers and families foster love and holiness through her intercession. R.

3. You gave Mary strength at the foot of the cross and filled her with joy at the resurrection of your Son,
   lighten the hardships of those who are burdened and deepen their sense of hope. R.

4. You made Mary open to your word and faithful as your servant,
   through her intercession make us servants and true followers of your Son. R.

5. You crowned Mary queen of heaven,
   may all the dead rejoice in your kingdom with the saints for ever. R.

B. "Akathist Hymn"

The minister or another person proclaims the acclamations:

Hail Mary! Hail, the restoration of the fallen Adam!
   Hail, the redemption of the tears of Eve.

All respond:

Intercede for us with the Lord.

Hail Mary! Height, hard to climb, for human minds;
Hail, depth, hard to explore, even for the eyes of angels. R.

Hail Mary! Throne of wisdom;
Hail, security and hope for all who call upon you. R.

Hail Mary! Heavenly ladder by which God came down to earth;
Hail, bridge leading from earth to heaven. R.

Hail Mary! Favor of God to mortals;
Hail, Mary, access of mortals to God. R.

Hail Mary! Mother of the Lamb and of the Good Shepherd;
Hail, fold for the sheep of his pasture. R.

Hail Mary! Never silent voice of the apostles;
Hail, never conquered courage of champions. R.

Hail Mary! Mother of the Star which never sets;
Hail, dawn of the mystic day. R.

Hail Mary! Guide of the wisdom of the faithful;
Hail, joy of all generations. R.

Let us pause and in the secrecy of our hearts present our special needs and
petitions to the Mother of Jesus.

After a brief pause the minister continues:

Hail Mary! Mother of God's only Son;
Hail, Mother of the Church. R.

PRAYER TO MARY

32. The following prayer to Mary is said. A traditional novena prayer to Mary may
replace the prayer.

The minister says:

We turn to you for protection,
holy Mother of God.

All then say:

Listen to our prayers

and help us in our needs.
Save us from every danger,
glorious and blessed Virgin.

DISMISSAL

33. The minister concludes with these words:

Be confident of Mary's intercession with her Son;
be confident that anyone who turns to her for help
    will never be left unaided.
Go now in her Son's peace.

All respond:

Thanks be to God.

34. The celebration should end with a song.

Procession with an Image of the Blessed Virgin Mary

Introduction

35. This service is intended for solemnities and feasts of the Blessed Virgin Mary when, as a form of homage, her image is carried in procession.

36. The rite consists of a liturgy of the word, the procession, and intercessions.

37. The service may be led by a priest, deacon, or lay person.

Procession with an
Image of the Blessed Virgin Mary

38. When all have gathered, a suitable song may be sung. The minister makes the sign of the cross, saying:

In the name of the Father, and of the Son, and of the Holy Spirit.

All respond:

Amen.

GREETING

39. The minister greets those present in the following or other suitable words, taken mainly from sacred Scripture:

Praise be to Jesus Christ, who was made flesh in the womb of the Virgin Mary. Blessed be God for ever.

All respond:

Blessed be God for ever.

INTRODUCTION

40. The minister introduces the celebration in these or similar words:

When the angel of the Lord proclaimed to Mary the good news of our salvation in Christ, she received God's Word with joy and welcomed her Son as Savior and Lord. As she stood beneath the cross and looked upon her suffering Son, she too experienced pain and sorrow. When she was raised to heaven, she shared the glory promised by her Son. Let us now acknowledge the mystery of God's love in Christ as we honor Mary, the Virgin Mother of God.

OPENING PRAYER

41. The minister says the opening prayer. On solemnities and feasts, the opening prayer of the Mass of the day or one of the prayers in no. 111 may be chosen.

Let us pray.

After a brief period of silent prayer, the minister continues:

Father,
source of light in every age,
the Virgin conceived and bore your Son
who is called Wonderful God, Prince of Peace.

May her prayer, the gift of a mother's love,
be your people's joy through all ages.
May her response, born of a humble heart,
draw your Spirit to rest on your people.

Grant this through Christ our Lord.

All respond:

Amen.

All sit.

READING FROM THE WORD OF GOD

42. A reader then proclaims the first reading from sacred Scripture. Additional readings are given in no. 115.

Galatians 4:4-7
God sent his Son, born of a woman.

A reading from the letter of Paul to the Galatians.

When the designated time had come, God sent forth his Son born of a woman, born under the law, to deliver from the law those who were subjected to it, so that we might receive our status as adopted sons. The proof that you are sons is the fact that God has sent forth into our hearts the spirit of his Son which cries out "Abba!" ("Father!") You are no longer a slave but a son! And the fact that you are a son makes you an heir, by God's design.

This is the Word of the Lord.

RESPONSORIAL PSALM

43. As circumstances suggest, one of the following responsorial psalms or some other suitable song may be sung:

Psalm 45:10,11,12,16

R. The queen stands at your right hand, arrayed in gold.

The queen takes her place at your right hand
  in gold of Ophir. R.

Hear, O daughter, and see; turn your ear,
  forget your people and your father's house. R.

So shall the king desire your beauty;
  for he is your lord. R.

They are borne in with gladness and joy;
  they enter the palace of the king. R.

NON-BIBLICAL READING

  44. A reader proclaims the following reading or one of those in no. 116:

  Pastoral Letter *Behold Your Mother: Woman of Faith*, National Conference of
  Catholic Bishops (November 21, 1973), nos. 81-82, "Mary in Our Life."

A reading from the Pastoral Letter of the National Conference of Catholic
Bishops, *Behold Your Mother: Woman of Faith.*

According to the *Constitution on the Sacred Liturgy*, the Church honors the
Mother of God when it celebrates the cycle of Christ's saving mysteries. For
"Blessed Mary is joined by an inseparable bond to the saving work of her
Son." Deeper Biblical insights have increased our awareness of Mary as the
model of faithful discipleship; but it is also our purpose here to reinforce our
Catholic sense of the Blessed Mother's present concern for us in her union
with the risen Christ.

Since early times, but especially after the Council of Ephesus, devotion to
Mary in the Church has grown wondrously. The People of God through the
ages have shown her veneration and love. They have called upon her in
prayer and they imitate her. All these ways of praising Mary draw us closer to
Christ. When Mary is honored, her Son is duly acknowledged, loved and
glorified, and His commandments are observed. To venerate Mary correctly
means to acknowledge her Son, for she is the Mother of God. To love her
means to love Jesus, for she is always the Mother of Jesus. To pray to our Lady
means not to substitute her for Christ, but to glorify her Son who desires us to
have loving confidence in His Saints, especially in His Mother. To imitate the
"faithful Virgin" means to keep her Son's commandments.

GOSPEL ACCLAMATION

  45. The gospel acclamation is sung.

Hail Mary, full of grace, the Lord is with you; blessed are you among women.
(Luke 1:28)

OR

Happy are you, holy Virgin Mary, deserving of all praise;
from you rose the sun of justice, Christ the Lord.

GOSPEL

> 46. The deacon (or, in his absence, the minister) proclaims the gospel. All stand during the gospel.

> Luke 11:27-28
> Happy the womb that bore you!

A reading from the holy gospel according to Luke.

While Jesus was speaking to the crowd a woman called out, "Blest is the womb that bore you and the beasts that nursed you!" "Rather," he replied, "blest are they who hear the word of God and keep it."

This is the gospel of the Lord.

> After the gospel, all sit during the homily.

HOMILY

> 47. The minister may give those present a brief explanation of the Scripture readings and the role of Mary in God's plan of salvation.

PROCESSION WITH THE IMAGE OF MARY

> 48. The procession with the statue or image of Mary takes place after the homily. During the procession, appropriate Marian acclamations or hymns may be sung. The Litany of Loreto may also be sung during the procession.

> The procession consists of ministers carrying the processional cross and candles, representatives of various parish or Marian organizations, the ministers, and the image of Mary.

> At the conclusion of the procession, the image of Mary is placed in a suitable place which is visible to the entire assembly.

INTERCESSIONS

> 49. The intercessions follow. In addition to the formulary below, the intercessions from Evening Prayer of the *Liturgy of the Hours* for a particular solemnity or feast may be used, or intentions may be composed for the occasion.

Let us praise God our almighty Father, who wished that Mary, his Son's mother, be celebrated by each generation. Now in need we ask:

R. Mary, full of grace, intercede for us.

1. O God, worker of miracles, you made the immaculate Virgin Mary share body and soul in your Son's glory in heaven, direct the hearts of your children to that same glory. R.

2. You made Mary our mother. Through her intercession grant strength to the weak, comfort to the sorrowing, pardon to sinners, salvation and peace to all. R.

3. You made Mary full of grace, grant all people the joyful abundance of your grace. R.

4. Make your Church of one mind and one heart in love, and help all those who believe to be one in prayer with Mary, the mother of Jesus. R.

5. You crowned Mary queen of heaven, may all the dead rejoice in your kingdom with the saints for ever. R.

LORD'S PRAYER

50. The minister introduces the Lord's Prayer:

Remember us, Lord, when you come to your kingdom and teach us how to pray:

All continue:

Our Father . . .

CONCLUDING PRAYER

51. The minister says the concluding prayer:

God of all times and seasons,
Lord of all ages,
hear the prayers of your people
who honor the Blessed Virgin Mary
as Mother and Queen.
Grant that by the grace of your Son

we may always serve you and our neighbors on earth
and be welcomed into your heavenly kingdom.

We ask this through Christ our Lord.

All respond:

Amen.

DISMISSAL

52. The minister says:

Let us always cherish Mary in our hearts and lives.

All respond:

For the Lord has looked with favor on his lowly servant.

Deacon (minister):

Go in the peace of Christ.

All respond:

Thanks be to God.

53. The celebration should end with a song.

Crowning an Image of the Blessed Virgin Mary

Introduction

54. "Both in the East and in the West the practice of depicting the Blessed Virgin Mary wearing a regal crown came into use in the era of the Council of Ephesus (A.D. 431). . . . It is especially from the end of the 16th century that in the West the practice became widespread for the faithful, both religious and laity, to crown images of the Blessed Virgin" (see *Order of Crowning an Image of the Blessed Virgin Mary*, nos. 3-4).

55. This service is intended for parish celebrations in which an image of the Blessed Virgin Mary, or one of the Blessed Virgin Mary and the infant Jesus, is to be crowned. The rite may be used appropriately as a part of May devotions to the Blessed Virgin Mary.

56. The service may be led by a priest, deacon, or lay person.

57. If there is to be a procession with the image of Mary, it should be well planned before the celebration begins. Appropriate Marian hymns may be sung during the procession and throughout the service (see no. 117 below).

Crowning an Image of the Blessed Virgin Mary

58. When all have gathered, a suitable song may be sung. The minister makes the sign of the cross, saying:

In the name of the Father, and of the Son, and of the Holy Spirit.

All respond:

Amen.

INVITATION TO PRAY

59. The minister invites those present to pray in these words:

Come, let us worship Christ, the Son of Mary.

All respond:

Let us give praise and thanks to the Lord
as we keep this day in loving memory of the Blessed Virgin Mary.

INTRODUCTION

60. The minister introduces the celebration in these or similar words:

My dear brothers and sisters:
We gather today to crown this image of the mother of Jesus (the Virgin Mary and her Son, our Lord Jesus Christ). As we acclaim Mary, the Mother of God, as our queen, and as the Mother of the Church, let us imitate her example and be attentive to the word of God. As we honor Mary, who is higher than the cherubim and yet like us, let us pray that through her intercession we may achieve holiness of life, and a deepened faith, hope, and love, as we seek to do the will of God in all things.

OPENING PRAYER

61. The minister says the opening prayer. Additional prayers are given in no. 111.

Let us pray.

After a brief period of silent prayer, he continues:

Father,
you have given us the mother of your Son
to be our queen and mother.
With the support of her prayers
may we come to share the glory of your children
in the kingdom of heaven.

We ask this through our Lord Jesus Christ, your Son,
who lives and reigns with you and the Holy Spirit,
one God, for ever and ever.

All respond:

Amen.

OR

During the Easter Season

Father,
as your Son was raised on the cross,
his mother Mary stood by him, sharing his sufferings.
May your Church be united with Christ
in his suffering and death
and so come to share in his rising to new life,
where he lives and reigns with you and the Holy Spirit,
one God, for ever and ever.

All respond:

Amen.

READING FROM THE WORD OF GOD

62. A reader then proclaims the first reading from sacred Scripture. The readings may be chosen from the texts that follow, from those given in no. 115, or from the texts assigned to one of the feasts of Mary.

1 Chronicles 15:3-4,15-16;16:1-2
They brought the ark of God in and put it inside the tent that David had pitched for it.

A reading from the first book of Chronicles.

David assembled all Israel in Jerusalem to bring the ark of the Lord to the place which he had prepared for it. David also called together the sons of Aaron and the Levites. The Levites bore the ark of God on their shoulders with poles, as Moses had ordained according to the Word of the Lord.

David commanded the chiefs of the Levites to appoint their brethren as chanters, to play on musical instruments, harps, lyres, and cymbals to make a loud sound of rejoicing.

They brought in the ark of God and set it within the tent which David had pitched for it. Then they offered up holocausts and peace offerings to God. When David had finished offering up the holocausts and peace offerings, he blessed the people in the name of the Lord.

This is the Word of the Lord.

During the Easter Season

> Revelation 11:19;12:1-6,10
> A great sign appeared in the heavens.

A reading from the book of Revelation.

God's temple in heaven opened and in the temple could be seen the ark of his covenant.

A great sign appeared in the sky, a woman clothed with the sun, with the moon under her feet, and on her head a crown of twelve stars. Because she was with child, she wailed aloud in pain as she labored to give birth. Then another sign appeared in the sky: it was a huge dragon, flaming red, with seven heads and ten horns; on his heads were seven diadems. His tail swept a third of the stars from the sky and hurled them down to the earth. Then the dragon stood before the woman about to give birth, ready to devour her child when it should be born. She gave birth to a son—a boy destined to shepherd all the nations with an iron rod. Her child was snatched up to God and to his throne. The woman herself fled into the desert, where a special place had been prepared for her by God.

Then I heard a loud voice in heaven say:

"Now have salvation and power come,
the reign of our God and the authority of his Anointed One."

This is the Word of the Lord.

RESPONSORIAL PSALM

63. As circumstances suggest, the following responsorial psalm or some other suitable song may be sung:

1 Samuel 2:1,4-5,6-7,8

R. My heart rejoices in the Lord, my Savior.

As Hannah worshiped the Lord, she said:
"My heart exults in the Lord,
   my horn is exalted in my God.
I have swallowed up my enemies;
   I rejoice in my victory." R.

The bows of the mighty are broken,
   while the tottering gird on strength.
The well-fed hire themselves out for bread,
   while the hungry batten on spoil.
The barren wife bears seven sons,
   while the mother of many languishes. R.

The Lord puts to death and gives life;
   he casts down to the nether world;
   he raises up again.
The Lord makes poor and makes rich,
   he humbles, he also exalts. R.

He raises the needy from the dust;
   from the ash heap he lifts up the poor,
To seat them with nobles
   and make a glorious throne their heritage. R.

GOSPEL ACCLAMATION

64. One of the following verses is sung before the gospel:

Happy are you, holy Virgin Mary, deserving of all praise;
from you rose the sun of justice, Christ the Lord.

OR

Blessed is the Virgin Mary who kept the word of God,
and pondered it in her heart.

65. The deacon (or, in his absence, the minister) proclaims the gospel. Additional readings are given in no. 115. All stand.

Luke 1:26-38
You will conceive and bear a son.

A reading from the holy gospel according to Luke.

The angel Gabriel was sent from God to a town of Galilee named Nazareth, to a virgin betrothed to a man named Joseph, of the house of David. The virgin's name was Mary. Upon arriving, the angel said to her: "Rejoice, O highly favored daughter! The Lord is with you. Blessed are you among women." She was deeply troubled by his words, and wondered what his greeting meant. The angel went on to say to her: "Do not fear, Mary. You have found favor with God. You shall conceive and bear a son and give him the name Jesus. Great will be his dignity and he will be called Son of the Most High. The Lord God will give him the throne of David his father. He will rule over the house of Jacob forever and his reign will be without end."

Mary said to the angel, "How can this be since I do not know man?" The angel answered her: "The Holy Spirit will come upon you and the power of the Most High will overshadow you; hence, the holy offspring to be born will be called Son of God. Know that Elizabeth your kinswoman has conceived a son in her old age; she who was thought to be sterile is now in her sixth month, for nothing is impossible with God."

Mary said: "I am the maidservant of the Lord. Let it be done to me as you say." With that the angel left her.

This is the gospel of the Lord.

During the Easter Season

John 19:25-27
Woman, this is your son. This is your mother.

A reading from the holy gospel according to John.

Near the cross of Jesus there stood his mother, his mother's sister, Mary the wife of Clopas, and Mary Magdalene. Seeing his mother there with the disciple whom he loved, Jesus said to his mother, "Woman, there is your son." In turn, he said to the disciple, "There is your mother." From that hour onward, the disciple took her into his care.

This is the gospel of the Lord.

HOMILY

66. The minister may give those present a brief explanation of the Scripture readings and the role of Mary in God's plan of salvation, or one of the non-biblical readings in no. 116 may be read.

Rite of Crowning

THANKSGIVING AND INVOCATION

67. After the homily, the minister stands before the image of the Mother of God and alternates saying the prayer of thanksgiving and invocation with the congregation.

Minister:

Lord,
we bless you,
for you are full of mercy and justice:
you humble the proud
and exalt the lowly.

All respond:

You gave us the highest example
of your divine wisdom
in the mystery of the Word made flesh
and of his virgin Mother.

Minister:

Your Son,
humbled by death,
rose glorious at your right hand,
the King of all creation.

All respond:

The Virgin, who acknowledged herself to be a servant,
became the Mother of our Redeemer

and of those reborn in her Son.

Now, raised above the angels,
she prays for all:
the Queen of mercy and grace.

Minister:

Bless us as we crown this image
of the Mother of your Son (of Christ and his Mother).

All Respond:

We confess Christ to be the King of creation
and call upon Mary, our Queen.
May we walk in their likeness
spending ourselves for the sake of others.

Content with our place in this life
may we one day hear your voice
inviting us to take our place in heaven
and receive the crown of victory.

CROWNING

68. The minister or another person places the crown on the image of Mary. If the image is of both Mary and the infant Jesus, the image of Christ is crowned before that of the Virgin Mary.

As the image is crowned an appropriate song is sung.

LITANY OF THE BLESSED VIRGIN MARY

69. After the crowning, the Litany of the Blessed Virgin Mary is sung or recited. A cantor or other minister sings or recites the invocations and all respond.

Lord, have mercy	Lord, have mercy
Christ, have mercy	Christ, have mercy
Lord, have mercy	Lord, have mercy
God our Father in heaven	have mercy on us
God the Son, Redeemer of the world	have mercy on us
God the Holy Spirit	have mercy on us
Holy Trinity, one God	have mercy on us

Holy Mary	pray for us
Holy Mother of God	pray for us
Most honored of virgins	pray for us
Chosen daughter of the Father	pray for us
Mother of Christ the King	pray for us
Glory of the Holy Spirit	pray for us
Virgin daughter of Zion	pray for us
Virgin poor and humble	pray for us
Virgin gentle and obedient	pray for us
Handmaid of the Lord	pray for us
Mother of the Lord	pray for us
Helper of the Redeemer	pray for us
Full of grace	pray for us
Fountain of beauty	pray for us
Model of virtue	pray for us
Finest fruit of the redemption	pray for us
Perfect disciple of Christ	pray for us
Untarnished image of the Church	pray for us
Woman transformed	pray for us
Woman clothed with the sun	pray for us
Woman crowned with stars	pray for us
Gentle Lady	pray for us
Gracious Lady	pray for us
Our Lady	pray for us
Joy of Israel	pray for us
Splendor of the Church	pray for us
Pride of the human race	pray for us
Advocate of peace	pray for us
Minister of holiness	pray for us
Champion of God's people	pray for us
Queen of love	pray for us
Queen of mercy	pray for us
Queen of peace	pray for us

Queen of angels	pray for us
Queen of patriarchs and prophets	pray for us
Queen of apostles and martyrs	pray for us
Queen of confessors and virgins	pray for us
Queen of all saints	pray for us
Queen conceived without original sin	pray for us
Queen assumed into heaven	pray for us
Queen of all the earth	pray for us
Queen of heaven	pray for us
Queen of the universe	pray for us

Lamb of God, you take away the sins of the world	spare us, O Lord
Lamb of God, you take away the sins of the world	hear us, O Lord
Lamb of God, you take away the sins of the world	have mercy on us

Minister:

Pray for us, O glorious Mother of the Lord.

All respond:

That we may become worthy of the promises of Christ.

The minister concludes the litany with the following prayer:

God of mercy,
listen to the prayers of your servants
who have honored your handmaid Mary as mother and queen.
Grant that by your grace
we may serve you and our neighbor on earth
and be welcomed into your eternal kingdom.

We ask this through Christ our Lord.

All respond:

Amen.

DISMISSAL

70. After the litany the minister says:

Gracious Lord,
with love and devotion we have honored the holy Mother of God.
May she continue to intercede for us with Jesus Christ, her Son,
now and for ever.

All respond:

Amen.

A priest or deacon adds:

May almighty God bless you,
the Father, and the Son, + and the Holy Spirit.

All respond:

Amen.

71. The celebration should end with a song.

Celebration of the Rosary

Introduction

72. The use of the rosary arose in the Middle Ages as a popular form of devotion. Regarded as an offshoot of the liturgy, the rosary has been called "Our Lady's Psalter" because through it the faithful "were enabled to associate themselves with the whole Church's song of praise and intercession" (*Marialis cultus*, no. 48). In the rosary, through devout meditation, the mysteries of Christ are called to mind and the faithful are disposed to "celebrate the same mysteries in the rites of the liturgy and then to keep memory of them alive throughout the day" (ibid.).

73. This service provides a communal form for the recitation of the rosary. It may be led by a priest, deacon, or lay person. This service may also be used in the family celebration of the rosary.

74. Music is an integral part of this service, and Marian hymns may be sung at the points indicated in the rite (see no. 117 below).

75. In keeping with *Marialis cultus* (no. 40), an additional set of mysteries centered around the Eucharist are provided.

76. The postures of the congregation during this service may be according to local custom.

Celebration of the Rosary

77. When all have gathered, a suitable song may be sung. The minister makes the sign of the cross, saying:

In the name of the Father, and of the Son, and of the Holy Spirit.

All respond:

Amen.

ACCLAMATION OF PRAISE

78. The minister says:

Blessed are you, O Mary,
for the world's salvation came forth from you;
you rejoice with the Lord in glory for ever.

All respond:

Intercede for us with your Son.

INTRODUCTION

79. The minister introduces the celebration using these or similar words:

We gather in faith to reflect upon the (glorious *OR* joyful *OR* sorrowful) mysteries of our faith as we pray the rosary. We do so in union with Mary, the Mother of God, who bore Jesus "in her womb with a love beyond all telling." With Mary and all the saints, let us now turn to Christ, the light of the world and the salvation of all.

INTRODUCTORY PRAYERS

80. The minister invites all present to profess their baptismal faith:

Let us together profess the faith of our baptism.

All then recite the Apostles' Creed:

I believe in God, the Father almighty,
creator of heaven and earth.

I believe in Jesus Christ, his only Son, our Lord.
    He was conceived by the power of the Holy Spirit
        and born of the Virgin Mary.
    He suffered under Pontius Pilate,
        was crucified, died, and was buried.
    He descended to the dead.
    On the third day he rose again.
    He ascended into heaven,
        and is seated at the right hand of the Father.
    He will come again to judge the living and the dead.

I believe in the Holy Spirit,
    the holy catholic Church,
    the communion of saints,
    the forgiveness of sins,
    the resurrection of the body,
    and the life everlasting. Amen.

81. The Lord's Prayer is recited. The minister begins:

Our Father, who art in heaven,
hallowed be thy name;
thy kingdom come;
thy will be done on earth as it is in heaven.

All continue:

Give us this day our daily bread;
and forgive us our trespasses
as we forgive those who trespass against us;
and lead us not into temptation,
but deliver us from evil.
Amen.

82. The minister says:

Faith, hope, and love are the three basic virtues central to our relationship with God. Let us pray for their growth and development in our lives as dedicated followers of Christ.

The "Hail Mary" is then said three times.

83. The minister says:

Glory to the Father, and to the Son, and to the Holy Spirit.

All respond:

As it was in the beginning, is now, and will be for ever. Amen.

MYSTERIES OF THE ROSARY

84. It is traditional to say all five decades of one of the mysteries of the rosary. According to custom, the joyful mysteries are used on Mondays and Thursdays and on the Sundays of Advent; the sorrowful mysteries are used on Tuesdays and Fridays and on the Sundays of Lent; the glorious mysteries are used on Wednesdays and Saturdays and on the remaining Sundays of the year.

The minister announces each mystery and, if desired, another person or the minister may read a brief passage related to the mystery being recalled. The "Lord's Prayer," ten "Hail Mary's," and the "Glory to the Father" are said for each mystery.

Joyful Mysteries

1. Annunciation of the birth of Jesus to Mary by the angel Gabriel—Luke 1:26-38.
2. Visitation of Mary to her cousin Elizabeth—Luke 1:39-47.
3. Nativity of our Lord and Savior Jesus Christ—Luke 2:1-7.
4. Presentation of the infant Jesus in the Temple—Luke 2:22-32.
5. Finding of the Child Jesus in the Temple by Mary and Joseph—Luke 2:41-52.

Sorrowful Mysteries

1. Agony of Christ in the Garden—Mark 14:32-36.
2. Scourging of Jesus at the Pillar—John 18:28-38;19:1.
3. Placing of the crown of thorns on the head of Jesus—Mark 15:16-20.
4. Carrying the Cross by Jesus—John 19:12-16.
5. Crucifixion of our Lord Jesus Christ—Luke 23:33-34;39-46.

Glorious Mysteries

1. Resurrection of our Lord from the dead—Luke 24:1-6a.
2. Ascension of our Lord into heaven—Luke 24:50-53.
3. Descent of the Holy Spirit upon the apostles on Pentecost—Acts 2:1-4.
4. Assumption of the Blessed Virgin Mary into heaven—Song of Songs 2:8-14.
5. Coronation of the Virgin Mary—Revelation 12:1-6 or *Lumen Gentium* 69:2.

Eucharistic Mysteries (Optional Additional Mysteries)

1. Feeding of the Israelites with manna in the widerness—
   Exodus 16:2-4;12-15.
2. Ratification of the Covenant in the Blood of Sacrifice—
   Exodus 24:3-8.
3. Miracle of the multiplication of the loaves and fishes—Luke 9:11-17.
4. Institution of the Eucharist—1 Corinthians 11:23-26.
5. Appearance of Christ on the road to Emmaus—Luke 24:13-35.

> 85. At the end of each decade, the assembly may sing a Marian
> acclamation or song.

HOMILY

> 86. A brief homily that relates the mysteries of the rosary to the daily life of the
> Christian may be given.

> 87. A brief period of silent prayer may follow either the mysteries or the homily.

INTERCESSIONS

> 88. The intercessions may be taken from Evening Prayer of the Common of the Blessed
> Virgin Mary in the *Liturgy of the Hours* (see no. 106) or from those that follow. The
> minister introduces and concludes the intercessions; another person may offer the
> petitions.

A. Joyful Mysteries

As faithful servants of the word of God, we come before the Lord in humility
and pray:

> R. Hear us, Lord.

1. Mary responded in faith to the word of God; may that saving word
   continue to take root in our hearts, we pray: R.

2. Mary cared for the poor, the afflicted, and the sorrowing; may we respond
   in love to all who are in need, we pray: R.

3. A child was born to Mary, and a Son was given to her; may all mothers
   rejoice in the gift of their children, we pray: R.

4. Mary treasured in her heart all that happened to her; may we always
   cherish God's blessings to us and give thanks for God's everlasting love,
   we pray: R.

5. Jesus, Son of God and Son of Mary, advanced in wisdom, age, and grace; may all young people receive the gifts of truth, wisdom, and love, we pray: R.

B. *Sorrowful Mysteries*

In baptism, we have shared in the mystery of Christ's death and resurrection. Let us turn to our Redeemer as we pray:

R. Lord, sustain us with your love.

1. Jesus was obedient to his Father in all things, even to death on the cross; may we obey God in all that we do, we pray: R.

2. Jesus submitted to suffering and death out of love for us; may our love for him lead us to accept daily trials and inconveniences in service to others, we pray: R.

3. Jesus patiently accepted the mockery and scorn of those who persecuted him; may we find comfort in his words: "Blessed are those who are persecuted for holiness' sake; the reign of God is theirs," we pray: R.

4. Jesus bore the weight of the cross; may he give us the strength to shoulder the daily burdens of life, we pray: R.

5. The cross reveals God's judgment on the world and the kingship of Christ; may we share in his passion by a deeper spirit of repentance, we pray: R.

C. *Glorious Mysteries*

Let us call upon Christ the Lord, who died and rose again, and intercedes for us with the Father, saying:

R. Victorious King, hear us, we pray.

1. Lord of life, you triumphed over sin and death; destroy the power of sin and death in us, that we may live only for you, we pray: R.

2. King of glory, you promised to draw all things to yourself; do not allow us to be separated from you or your Church, we pray: R.

3. Lord the light of your Holy Spirit enlightens the world and dispels the darkness of the world; grant us the grace to turn hatred to love, sorrow to joy, and war into peace, we pray: R.

4. You exalted your Virgin Mother above all the choirs of angels; give us a share one day in the joy that is now hers in your kingdom, we pray: R.

5. You crowned your Mother as Queen of heaven and earth; set our hearts on the goal of reaching the heavenly Jerusalem, we pray: R.

D. Eucharistic Mysteries

Mary is the path that leads to Christ. Through her, we are brought to a deeper encounter with Christ, her Son. Let us now turn to Jesus and pray, Lord in your mercy:

R. Hear our prayer.

1. Lord, in the Father's plan, you were born of a woman under the law, that we might receive our adoption as God's children; may we continue to appreciate this divine mystery of love revealed to us in your Church. Lord in your mercy: R.

2. You were incarnate by the Holy Spirit of the Virgin Mary; grant us like Mary to be fitting vessels of your glory. Lord in your mercy: R.

3. We honor Mary as your Mother; grant that through her intercession we may be more closely united with you in the mystery of love. Lord in your mercy: R.

4. You give us Mary, your Mother, to be the Mother of your Church and the model of faith and charity; grant to us, your Church, a deeper fidelity and a greater love. Lord in your mercy: R.

5. Lord Jesus, you have raised Mary to your presence in glory, yet she remains close to your Church; remember us in your love. Lord in your mercy: R.

LORD'S PRAYER

89. After the intercessions, the minister introduces the Lord's Prayer in the following or similar words:

With Mary we call upon the Father in prayer.

All sing or recite the Lord's Prayer:

Our Father . . .

CONCLUDING PRAYER

90. The minister says the concluding prayer:

Pray for us, O holy Mother of God.

All respond:

That we may be made worthy of the promises of Christ.

The minister continues:

Lord,
fill our hearts with your grace:
once, through the message of an angel
you revealed to us the incarnation of your Son;
now, through his suffering and death
lead us to the glory of his resurrection.

We ask this through Christ our Lord.

All respond:

Amen.

OR

Father of Jesus and our Father,
we acknowledge your choice of Mary
to be the Mother of your only Son.
She is your favorite daughter
and became the temple of the Holy Spirit.
Look upon us in love
and mold us into the image of Christ Jesus.
He is Lord and lives and reigns with you and the Holy Spirit,
one God, for ever and ever.

All respond:

Amen.

BLESSING AND DISMISSAL

91. A priest or deacon may bless those present.

92. The minister concludes the rite with these words:

Let us go forth to be the light and peace of Christ in the world.

All respond:

In the name of Christ. Amen.

SALVE, REGINA

93. The Salve, Regina or another Marian antiphon (no. 112) or a hymn is sung.

Evening Prayer

Introduction

94. "The purpose of the liturgy of the hours is to sanctify the day and the whole range of human activity" (*General Instruction of the Liturgy of the Hours*, no. 11). Evening Prayer or Vespers is "celebrated in order that 'we may give thanks for what has been given us, or what we have done well, during the day' [see Basil the Great *Regulae fusius tractatae* resp. 37, 3: PG 31, 1015]. We also recall the redemption through the prayer we send up 'like incense in the Lord's sight,' and in which 'the raising up of our hands' becomes 'an evening sacrifice' " [see Ps 141:2] (GILH, no. 39).

95. This celebration of Evening Prayer is taken from the Common of the Blessed Virgin Mary of the *Liturgy of the Hours*. It may be celebrated on those days permitted by the *General Norms for the Liturgical Year and the Calendar*.

96. An image of the Blessed Virgin Mary may be placed in a suitable place visible to the entire assembly. Instrumental music may be played before the service begins. A Bible or other book containing the biblical reading may be carried in the entrance procession.

97. Evening Prayer may be led by a priest, deacon, or lay person.

Evening Prayer

98. The minister makes the sign of the cross and sings or says:

God, come to my assistance.

All respond:

Lord, make haste to help me.

Glory to the Father, and to the Son, and to the Holy Spirit:
as it was in the beginning, is now, and will be for ever.
Amen. (Alleluia.)

HYMN

99. A suitable Marian hymn is sung (see no. 117).

PSALMODY

100. The antiphon of each psalm may be sung by the cantor and repeated by the congregation at the beginning and end of the psalm. The antiphon may also be repeated after each strophe by the congregation.

The psalms may be sung as a single unit without a break; with two choirs or sections of the congregation singing alternate verses or strophes; or responsorially.

All are seated during the psalmody.

Ant. 1   Blessed are you, O Virgin Mary, for you carried
the Creator of the world in your womb.

Psalm 113

Praise, O servants of the Lord,
praise the name of the Lord!
May the name of the Lord be blessed
both now and for evermore!
From the rising of the sun to its setting
praised be the name of the Lord!

High above all nations is the Lord,
above the heavens his glory.
Who is like the Lord, our God,
who has risen on high to his throne
yet stoops from the heights to look down,
to look down upon heaven and earth?

From the dust he lifts up the lowly,
from his misery he raises the poor
to set him in the company of princes,
yes, with the princes of his people.
To the childless wife he gives a home
and gladdens her heart with children.

Glory to the Father, and to the Son, and to the Holy Spirit:
as it was in the beginning, is now, and will be for ever. Amen.

Ant.   Blessed are you, O Virgin Mary, for you carried
the Creator of the world in your womb.

Ant. 2   You are the mother of your Maker,
yet you remain a virgin for ever.

Psalm 147:12-20

O praise the Lord, Jerusalem!
Zion, praise your God!

He has strengthened the bars of your gates,
he has blessed the children within you.
He has established peace on your borders,
he feeds you with finest wheat.

He sends out his word to the earth
and swiftly runs his command.
He showers down snow white as wool,
he scatters hoar-frost like ashes.

He hurls down hailstones like crumbs.
The waters are frozen at his touch;
he sends forth his word and it melts them:
at the breath of his mouth the waters flow.

He makes his word known to Jacob,
to Israel his laws and decrees.
He has not dealt thus with other nations;
he has not taught them his decrees.

Glory to the Father, and to the Son, and to the Holy Spirit:
as it was in the beginning, is now, and will be for ever. Amen.

Ant.   You are the mother of your Maker,
         yet you remain a virgin for ever.

Ant. 3   We share the fruit of life through you,
         O daughter blessed by the Lord.

Canticle Ephesians 1:3-10

Praised be the God and Father
of our Lord Jesus Christ,
who bestowed on us in Christ
every spiritual blessing in the heavens.

God chose us in him
before the world began,
to be holy
and blameless in his sight.

He predestined us
to be his adopted sons through Jesus Christ,
such was his will and pleasure,
that all might praise the glorious favor
he has bestowed on us in his beloved.

In him and through his blood, we have been redeemed,
and our sins forgiven,
so immeasurably generous
is God's favor to us.

God has given us the wisdom
to understand fully the mystery,
the plan he was pleased
to decree in Christ.

A plan to be carried out
in Christ, in the fullness of time,
to bring all things into one in him,
in the heavens and on the earth.

Glory to the Father, and to the Son, and to the Holy Spirit:
as it was in the beginning, is now, and will be for ever. Amen.

Ant.   We share the fruit of life through you,
         O daughter blessed by the Lord.

READING

101. A reader proclaims the reading from sacred Scripture. One of the following readings, the reading assigned to the solemnity or feast, or one of those given in no. 115 may be chosen.

Proverbs 8:22-31
Mary, seat of wisdom.

A reading from the book of Proverbs.

[Thus speaks the Wisdom of God:]
"The Lord begot me, the firstborn of his ways,
    the forerunner of his prodigies of long ago;
From of old I was poured forth,
    at the first, before the earth.
When there were no depths I was brought forth,
    when there were no fountains of springs of water;
Before the mountains were settled into place,
    before the hills, I was brought forth;
While as yet the earth and the fields were not made,
    nor the first clods of the world.

"When he established the heavens I was there,
    when he marked out the vault over the face of the deep;
When he made firm the skies above,
    when he fixed fast the foundations of the earth;
When he set for the sea its limit,
    so that the waters should not transgress his command;
Then was I beside him as his craftsman,
    and I was his delight day by day,
Playing before him all the while,
    playing on the surface of his earth;
    [and I found delight in the sons of men.]"

This is the Word of the Lord.

Easter Season

Revelation 21:1-5
I saw the new Jerusalem, as beautiful as a bride all dressed for her husband.

A reading from the book of Revelation.

I, John, saw new heavens and a new earth. The former heavens and the former earth had passed away, and the sea was no longer. I also saw a new Jerusalem, the holy city, coming down out of heaven from God, beautiful as a bride prepared to meet her husband. I heard a loud voice from the throne cry out: "This is God's dwelling among men. He shall dwell with them and they shall be his people, and he shall be their God who is always with them. He shall wipe every tear from their eyes, and there shall be no more death or mourning, crying out or pain, for the former world has passed away."

The One who sat on the throne said to me, "See, I make all things new!"

This is the Word of the Lord.

102. The reading may be followed by a period of silent reflection.

HOMILY

103. A brief homily may be given, or one of the non-biblical readings in no. 115 may be read.

RESPONSORY

104. The responsory is then sung.

Cantor:

After the birth of your son, you remained a virgin.

All respond:

After the birth of your son, you remained a virgin.

Cantor:

Mother of God, intercede for us;

All respond:

you remained a virgin.

Cantor:

Glory to the Father, and to the Son, and to the Holy Spirit.

All respond:

After the birth of your son, you remained a virgin.

CANTICLE OF MARY

> 105. During the antiphon, a priest or deacon may put incense in the censer and incense the altar, cross (image of Mary), and congregation during the Canticle of Mary. During the Canticle, all stand.

Ant.   The Lord has looked with favor on his lowly servant;
the Almighty has done great things for me.

OR

Blessed are you, O Virgin Mary, for your great faith;
all that the Lord promised you will come to pass through you.

Canticle of Mary   Luke 1:46-55

My soul proclaims the greatness of the Lord,
my spirit rejoices in God my Savior
for he has looked with favor on his lowly servant.

From this day all generations will call me blessed:
the Almighty has done great things for me,
and holy is his Name.

He has mercy on those who fear him
in every generation.

He has shown the strength of his arm,
he has scattered the proud in their conceit.

He has cast down the mighty from their thrones,
and has lifted up the lowly.

He has filled the hungry with good things,
and the rich he has sent away empty.

He has come to the help of his servant Israel
for he has remembered his promise of mercy,
the promise he made to our fathers,
to Abraham and his children for ever.

Glory to the Father, and to the Son, and to the Holy Spirit:
as it was in the beginning, is now, and will be for ever. Amen.

Ant.   The Lord has looked with favor on his lowly servant;
            the Almighty has done great things for me.

OR

            Blessed are you, O Virgin Mary, for your great faith;
            all that the Lord promised you will come to pass through you.

INTERCESSIONS

106. The intercessions are introduced by the minister; the intentions are proclaimed by another person. Other suitable intentions may be added to those given here. All stand for the intercessions and the remainder of the service.

Let us praise God our almighty Father, who wished that Mary, his Son's mother, be celebrated by each generation. Now in need we ask:

R. Mary, full of grace, intercede for us.

1. O God, worker of miracles, you made the immaculate Virgin Mary share body and soul in your Son's glory in heaven,
   direct the hearts of your children to that same glory. R.

2. You made Mary our mother. Through her intercession grant strength to the weak, comfort to the sorrowing, pardon to sinners,
   salvation and peace to all. R.

3. You made Mary full of grace,
   grant all people the joyful abundance of your grace. R.

4. Make your Church of one mind and one heart in love,
   and help all those who believe to be one in prayer with Mary, the mother of Jesus. R.

5. You crowned Mary queen of heaven,
   may all the dead rejoice in your kingdom with the saints for ever. R.

LORD'S PRAYER

107. The minister introduces the Lord's Prayer:

Gathering our prayers and praises into one, let us offer the prayer Christ himself taught us.

All continue:

Our Father . . .

CONCLUDING PRAYER

108. The minister says the concluding prayer:

God of mercy,
give us strength.
May we who honor the memory of the Mother of God
rise above our sins and failings with the help of her prayers.

Grant this through our Lord Jesus Christ, your Son,
who lives and reigns with you and the Holy Spirit,
one God, for ever and ever.

All respond:

Amen.

DISMISSAL

109. If a priest or deacon presides, he dismisses the people:

The Lord be with you.

All respond:

And also with you.

He continues:

May almighty God bless you,
the Father, and the Son, + and the Holy Spirit.

All respond:

Amen.

Another form of the blessing may be used, as at Mass. Then he adds:

Go in peace.

All respond:

Thanks be to God.

In the absence of a priest or deacon, Evening Prayer concludes:

May the Lord bless us,
protect us from all evil
and bring us to everlasting life.

All respond:

Amen.

Prayers in Honor of the
Blessed Virgin Mary

110. Over the course of centuries, many prayers honoring Mary or addressed directly to her have been written. Many are based on Scripture, such as the "Hail Mary." Others are rooted in ancient devotions or other forms of popular piety. Still others were written by saints who were especially devoted to the Mother of God. In this section, many of the ancient and modern prayers are provided for private devotion, while other prayers and antiphons are commended for use in public devotion. This collection by no means exhausts the vast treasury of Marian prayer.

Opening Prayers

111. The following Opening Prayers (collects) from the Italian Missal (*Messale Romano*) may be used in any of the celebrations contained in this collection:

A. Lord our God,
  you have made the Virgin Mary
  the model for all who welcome your word
  and who put it into practice.
  Open our hearts to receive it with joy
  and by the power of your Spirit
  grant that we also may become a dwelling place
  in which your Word of salvation is fulfilled.

  We ask this through our Lord Jesus Christ, your Son,
  who lives and reigns with you and the Holy Spirit,
  one God, for ever and ever.

B. Eternal Father,
  you have established in the Virgin Mary
  the royal throne of your Wisdom.
  Enlighten the Church by the Word of life,
  that we may walk in the splendor of truth
  and come to full knowledge of your mystery of love.

  Grant this through our Lord Jesus Christ, your Son,
  who lives and reigns with you and the Holy Spirit,
  one God, for ever and ever.

C. God our Father,
  as a root springs forth from fertile soil
  so Christ, your Son, by the power of your grace,
  was delivered of the Virgin Mary.
  Grant that every Christian,
  grafted to him through baptism in the Spirit,
  may be renewed in youth
  and be given the first fruits of grace
    to praise your glory for ever.

We ask this through our Lord Jesus Christ, your Son,
who lives and reigns with you and the Holy Spirit,
one God, for ever and ever.

D. Holy and merciful God,
   you are pleased by the humble
   and accomplish in them by means of the Spirit
   the great wonders of salvation.
   Look upon the innocence of the Virgin Mary,
   and give us simple and generous hearts
   that respond without hesitation to every sign of your will.

   Grant this through our Lord Jesus Christ, your Son,
   who lives and reigns with you and the Holy Spirit,
   one God, for ever and ever.

E. God and Father of the Lord Jesus Christ,
   look upon the Virgin Mary,
   whose earthly existence was governed
   by a spirit of gracious acceptance.
   Grant to us also
   the gifts of constant prayer and of silence,
   that our daily lives may be transfigured
   by the presence of your Spirit.

   We ask this through our Lord Jesus Christ, your Son,
   who lives and reigns with you and the Holy Spirit,
   one God, for ever and ever.

F. Father of holiness,
   for the journey of your pilgrim Church on earth,
   you have provided the Virgin Mary as a sign and beacon.
   Through her intercession
   sustain our faith and enliven our hope,
   that no obstacle may divert us
   from the road which brings us salvation.

   Grant this through our Lord Jesus Christ, your Son,
   who lives and reigns with you and the Holy Spirit,
   one God, for ever and ever.

G. Gracious God and Father,
   in Mary, the first-born of redemption,
   you have given us a Mother most tender.
   Open our hearts to the joy of the Spirit,
   and grant that by imitating the Virgin
   we too may learn to magnify you
   through the great work accomplished in Christ, your Son.
   He lives and reigns with you and the Holy Spirit,
   one God, for ever and ever.

H. Lord our God,
   you desired that the Mother of your Son
   should be present and joined in prayer
   with the first Christian community.
   Grant us the grace
   to persevere with her in awaiting the Spirit,
   that we may be one in heart and mind
   and come to taste
   the sweet and enduring fruits of redemption.

   We ask this through our Lord Jesus Christ, your Son,
   who lives and reigns with you and the Holy Spirit,
   one God, for ever and ever.

I. God of eternal glory,
   in Christ your Son, sprung from a Virgin Mother,
   you have brought true joy to the world.
   Free us from the weight of sin
   that saddens and extinguishes your Spirit,
   and welcome us to the table of your kingdom
   where you satisfy us with the bread that contains all sweetness.

   We ask this through our Lord Jesus Christ, your Son,
   who lives and reigns with you and the Holy Spirit,
   one God, for ever and ever.

J. God and Father of Christ our Savior,
   in Mary, the holy Virgin and attentive Mother,
   you have given us the image of your Church.
   Send your Spirit to help our weakness,
   that we may persevere in faith, grow in love,
   and walk together to the heaven of blessed hope.

We ask this through our Lord Jesus Christ, your Son,
who lives and reigns with you and the Holy Spirit,
one God, for ever and ever.

Antiphons of the Blessed Virgin Mary

112. The following antiphons of the Blessed Virgin Mary may be sung at the conclusion of any of the services in this book. They may also be used in private prayer.

ALMA REDEMPTORIS MATER

The "Alma Redemptoris Mater," which dates from the eleventh century, is one of the four antiphons sung after Night Prayer. It is used in the Advent Season.

Loving mother of the Redeemer,
gate of heaven, star of the sea,
assist your people who have fallen yet strive to rise again.
To the wonderment of nature you bore your Creator,
yet remained a virgin after as before.
You who received Gabriel's joyful greeting,
have pity on us poor sinners.

> Alma Redemptoris Mater, quae pervia caeli
> porta manes, et stella maris, succurre cadenti,
> surgere qui curat, populo: tu quae genuisti,
> natura mirante, tuum sanctum Genitorem,
> Virgo prius ac posterius, Gabrielis ab ore
> summens illud Ave, peccatorum miserere.

AVE REGINA CAELORUM

The "Ave Regina Caelorum" is one of the four antiphons sung after Night Prayer. It is used in Lent.

Hail, Queen of heaven;
Hail, Mistress of the Angels;
Hail, root of Jesse;
Hail, the gate through which the Light rose over the earth.
Rejoice, Virgin most renowned and of unsurpassed beauty.

> Ave, Regina caelorum,
> ave, Domina angelorum,
> salve, radix, salve, porta,
> ex qua mundo lux est orta.

Gaude, Virgo gloriosa,
super omnes speciosa;
vale, o valde decora,
et pro nobis Christum exora.

REGINA CAELI

The "Regina Caeli" is a twelfth-century antiphon for Evening Prayer during the Easter Season. Since the thirteenth century, it has been used as the seasonal antiphon in honor of the Blessed Virgin after Night Prayer.

Queen of heaven, rejoice, alleluia.
The Son whom you merited to bear, alleluia,
has risen as he said, alleluia.
Pray to God for us, alleluia.

Rejoice and be glad, O Virgin Mary, alleluia.
For the Lord has truly risen, alleluia.

Regina caeli, laetare, alleluia:
quia quem meruisti portare, alleluia.
Resurrexit, sicut dixit, alleluia.
Ora pro nobis Deum, alleluia.

Gaude et laetare, Virgo Maria, alleluia.
Quia surrexit Dominus vere, alleluia.

SALVE, REGINA

The "Salve, Regina" is one of the four Marian antiphons sung at the end of Night Prayer, according to the season. It was possibly written by Hermann the Lame, a monk of Reichenau (1013-1054), or by Adhemar, bishop of Le Puy (d. 1098). The "Salve, Regina" was also used as a processional antiphon at the Abbey of Cluny (France) from around 1135.

Hail, holy Queen, Mother of mercy,
hail, our life, our sweetness, and our hope.
To you we cry, the children of Eve;
to you we send up our sighs,
mourning and weeping in this land of exile.
Turn, then, most gracious advocate,
your eyes of mercy toward us;
lead us home at last
and show us the blessed fruit of your womb, Jesus:
O clement, O loving, O sweet Virgin Mary.

Salve, Regina, mater misericordiae;
vita, dulcedo et spes nostra, salve.
Ad te clamamus, exsules filii Evae.
Ad te suspiramus, gementes et flentes
in hac lacrimarum valle.

Eia ergo, advocata nostra,
illos tuos misericordes oculos ad nos converte.
Et Iesum, benedictum fructum ventris tui,
nobis post hoc exsilium ostende.
O clemens, o pia, o dulcis Virgo Maria.

Prayers to the Blessed Virgin Mary

113. The following prayers are suitable for private prayer. They may also be adapted for use in one of the services contained in this book.

THE ANGELIC SALUTATION

The "Hail Mary" ("Ave Maria") is based on Luke 1:28,42 and is known as the "Angelic Salutation" from the first line of the prayer.

Hail Mary, full of grace,
the Lord is with you!
Blessed are you among women,
and blessed is the fruit of your womb, Jesus.
Holy Mary, Mother of God,
pray for us sinners,
now and at the hour of our death.
Amen.

Ave Maria,
gratia plena, Dominus tecum,
benedicta tu in mulieribus,
et benedictus fructus ventris tui, Iesus.
Sancta Maria, Mater Dei,
ora pro nobis peccatoribus,
nunc et in hora mortis nostrae.
Amen.

CANTICLE OF MARY

The "Canticle of Mary" or "Magnificat" is sung in the celebration of Evening Prayer each day. The text is taken from the Gospel according to Luke 2:29-32.

My soul proclaims the greatness of the Lord,
my spirit rejoices in God my Savior
for he has looked with favor on his lowly servant.

From this day all generations will call me blessed:
the Almighty has done great things for me,
and holy is his Name.

He has mercy on those who fear him
in every generation.

He has shown the strength of his arm,
he has scattered the proud in their conceit.

He has cast down the mighty from their thrones,
and has lifted up the lowly.

He has filled the hungry with good things,
and the rich he has sent away empty.

He has come to the help of his servant Israel
for he remembered his promise of mercy,
the promise he made to our fathers,
to Abraham and his children for ever.

THE ANGELUS

The custom of saying the "Hail Mary" three times at the ringing of the bell in the evening goes back to the thirteenth century. Bells from that period were often inscribed with the the angelic salutation. Today, it is the custom to say the "Angelus" three times: in the morning, at noon, and in the evening. The collect was formerly the postcommunion for Masses of our Lady in Advent and is now the opening prayer for the Fourth Sunday of Advent.

V. The angel spoke God's message to Mary,
R. and she conceived of the Holy Spirit.

Hail Mary . . .

V. "I am the lowly servant of the Lord:
R. Let it be done to me according to your word."

Hail Mary . . .

V. And the Word became flesh
R. and lived among us.

Hail Mary . . .

V. Pray for us, holy Mother of God,
R. that we may become worthy of the promises of Christ.

Let us pray:

Lord,
fill our hearts with your grace:
once, through the message of an angel
you revealed to us the incarnation of your Son;
now, through his suffering and death
lead us to the glory of his resurrection.
We ask this through Christ our Lord.

R. Amen.

REGINA CAELI

The "Regina Caeli" is a twelfth-century antiphon for Evening Prayer during the Easter Season. Since the thirteenth century, it has been used as the seasonal antiphon in honor of the Blessed Virgin after Night Prayer. From 1743, it has replaced the Angelus in the Easter Season.

Queen of heaven, rejoice, alleluia.
The Son whom you merited to bear, alleluia,
has risen as he said, alleluia.
Pray to God for us, alleluia.

V. Rejoice and be glad, O Virgin Mary, alleluia.
R. For the Lord has truly risen, alleluia.

Let us pray.

God of life,
you have given joy to the world
by the resurrection of your Son, our Lord Jesus Christ.
Through the prayers of his mother, the Virgin Mary,
bring us to the happiness of eternal life.
We ask this through Christ our Lord.

R. Amen.

Regina caeli, laetare, alleluia:
quia quem meruisti portare, alleluia.
Resurrexit, sicut dixit, alleluia.
Ora pro nobis Deum, alleluia.

Gaude et laetare, Virgo Maria, alleluia.
Quia surrexit Dominus vere, alleluia.

SUB TUUM PRAESIDUM, ANCIENT PRAYER TO THE VIRGIN

This prayer, known in Latin as "Sub tuum praesidium" and first found in a Greek papyrus, c. 300, is the oldest known prayer to the Virgin.

We turn to you for protection,
holy Mother of God.
Listen to our prayers
and help us in our needs.
Save us from every danger,
glorious and blessed Virgin.

MEMORARE

The "Memorare" is a sixteenth-century version of a fifteenth-century prayer that began "Ad sanctitatis tuae pedes, dulcissima Virgo Maria." Claude Bernard (1588-1641) popularized the idea that the "Memorare" was written by Saint Bernard.

Remember, most loving Virgin Mary,
never was it heard
that anyone who turned to you for help
was left unaided.

Inspired by this confidence,
though burdened by my sins,
I run to your protection
for you are my mother.

Mother of the Word of God,
do not despise my words of pleading
but be merciful and hear my prayer.
Amen.

MARY, HELP OF THOSE IN NEED

"Mary, Help of Those in Need" was formerly the Magnificat antiphon from the Common of the Blessed Virgin Mary, Evening Prayer.

Holy Mary,
help those in need,
give strength to the weak,
comfort the sorrowful,
pray for God's people,
assist the clergy,
intercede for religious.

May all who seek your help
experience your unfailing protection.
Amen.

OUR LADY OF GUADALUPE

In the dioceses of the United States of America, Our Lady of Guadalupe is celebrated on December 12. The following is the Opening Prayer of the memorial of Our Lady of Guadalupe.

God of power and mercy,
you blessed the Americas at Tepeyac
with the presence of the Virgin Mary of Guadalupe.
May her prayers help all men and women
to accept each other as brothers and sisters.

Through your justice present in our hearts
may your peace reign in the world.

We ask this through our Lord Jesus Christ, your Son,
who lives and reigns with you and the Holy Spirit,
one God, for ever and ever.

Amen.

A CHILD'S PRAYER TO MARY

This prayer is from the hymn "Memento rerum conditor." It is also found as the last verse in some versions of the hymn "Quem terra pontus aethera."

Mary, mother whom we bless,
full of grace and tenderness,
defend me from the devil's power
and greet me in my dying hour.

A PRAYER FOR VOCATIONS

This prayer was prepared by the Secretariat of the Bishops' Committee on Vocations, National Conference of Catholic Bishops, in 1987.

Hail Mary, full of grace;
all generations call you blessed.

Hail Mother of God; when asked by the angel
    to bear the Son of the Most High,
    filled with faith, you responded:
    "Let it be done unto me."

Holy Mother of Jesus, at the wedding feast at Cana,
    you prompted your Son to perform his first sign.

    Be with us as we discern our life's work
    and guide us in the way we are called to follow
    in the footsteps of your Son.

Holy Mother of the Savior, at the foot of the cross
    you mourned the death of your only Son.

    Bless and embrace the loving parents of all priests,
    deacons, brothers, and sisters.

Holy Mother of the Good Shepherd,
    turn your motherly care to this nation.

    Intercede for us to the Lord of the harvest
    to send more laborers to the harvest
    in this land dedicated to your honor.

Queen of Peace, Mirror of Justice, Health of the Sick,
    inspire vocations in our time.

    Let the word of your Son be made flesh anew
    in the lives of persons anxious to proclaim
    the good news of everlasting life.

Amen.

A PRAYER FROM THE MARONITE LITURGY

The following prayer is taken from "Ramsho" or Evening Prayer (Common of the Blessed Virgin Mary) from the Prayer of the Faithful or Divine Office of the Syriac Maronite Antiochene Church.

Father,
author of all goodness,
we adore you who gave Mary the grace of innocence
    from the time of her conception.
O Son and Word eternal,
we exalt you who appeared in time for our salvation as
    the Son of Mary.
O Holy Spirit, glory be to you who chose Mary as your spouse,
for by you all generations proclaim her blessed.

O God,
through her intercession keep us from all harm
and let us always do good by keeping your commandments
    and by pleasing you.
With her we will praise you for ever.
Amen.

A HYMN OF PRAISE TO MARY FROM THE BYZANTINE LITURGY

*This hymn of praise known as the "Megalynarion" (or "Great Hymn to the Theotokos")
is taken from the Divine Liturgy of Saint John Chrysostom of the Byzantine Rite.*

It is proper to call you blessed,
ever-esteemed Theotokos, most pure, and mother of God.
You who are more worthy of honor than the cherubim
and far more glorious than the seraphim.
You who incorruptibly gave birth to God the Word,
verily Theotokos, we fervently extol you.

A PRAYER TO MARY FROM THE ACT OF ENTRUSTING THE WORLD TO MARY BY POPE JOHN PAUL II

Hail to you, Mary,
who are wholly united to the redeeming consecration of your Son!

Mother of the Church,
enlighten the people of God along the paths of faith, hope, and love.
Help us to live in the truth of the consecration of Christ
for the entire human family of the modern world.

In entrusting to you, O Mother,
the world, all individuals and peoples,
we also entrust to you this very consecration of the world,
placing it in your motherly heart.

Immaculate Heart of Mary,
help us to conquer the menace of evil,
which so easily takes root in the hearts of the people of today,
and whose immeasurable effects
already weigh down upon our modern world
and seem to block the paths toward the future.

    From famine and war, deliver us.
    From nuclear war, from incalculable self-destruction, from every kind
        of war, deliver us.
    From sins against human life from its very beginning, deliver us.

From hatred and from the demeaning of the dignity of the children
  of God, deliver us.
From every kind of injustice in the life of society,
  both national and international, deliver us.
From readiness to trample on the commandments of God, deliver us.
From attempts to stifle in human hearts the very truth of God,
  deliver us.
From the loss of awareness of good and evil, deliver us.
From sins against the Holy Spirit, deliver us.

Accept, O Mother of Christ,
this cry laden with the sufferings of all individual human beings,
laden with the sufferings of whole societies.

Help us with the power of the Holy Spirit to conquer all sin:
  individual sin and the "sin of the world,"
  sin in all its manifestations.
Let there be revealed once more in the history of the world
the infinite saving power of the redemption:
  the power of merciful love.
May it put a stop to evil.
May it transform consciences.
May your immaculate heart reveal for all the light of hope.

Amen.

PRAYER TO SAINT JOSEPH

While the Fathers of the Church praised Saint Joseph in their writings, devotion to the husband of Mary arose in the Western Church only in the fifteenth century. Pope Leo XIII (1810-1903) encouraged the recitation of this prayer after the rosary and the Litany of Loreto during the month of October.

Blessed Joseph, husband of Mary, be with us this day.

You protected and cherished the Virgin;
loving the Child Jesus as your Son,
you rescued him from danger of death.
Defend the Church, the household of God,
purchased by the blood of Christ.

Guardian of the holy family,
be with us in our trials.
May your prayers obtain for us
the strength to flee from error

and wrestle with the powers of corruption
so that in life we may grow in holiness
and in death rejoice in the crown of victory.

Amen.

LITANY OF SAINT JOSEPH

The following Litany of Saint Joseph was approved for devotional use by Pope Saint Pius X (1835-1914).

Lord, have mercy	Lord, have mercy
Christ, have mercy	Christ, have mercy
Lord, have mercy	Lord, have mercy
God our Father in heaven	have mercy on us
God the Son, Redeemer of the world	have mercy on us
God the Holy Spirit	have mercy on us
Holy Trinity, one God	have mercy on us
Holy Mary	pray for us
Saint Joseph	pray for us
Noble son of the House of David	pray for us
Light of patriarchs	pray for us
Husband of the Mother of God	pray for us
Guardian of the Virgin	pray for us
Foster father of the Son of God	pray for us
Faithful guardian of Christ	pray for us
Head of the holy family	pray for us
Joseph, chaste and just	pray for us
Joseph, prudent and brave	pray for us
Joseph, obedient and loyal	pray for us
Pattern of patience	pray for us
Lover of poverty	pray for us
Model of workers	pray for us
Example to parents	pray for us
Guardian of virgins	pray for us
Pillar of family life	pray for us
Comfort of the troubled	pray for us
Hope of the sick	pray for us
Patron of the dying	pray for us
Terror of evil spirits	pray for us
Protector of the Church	pray for us

Lamb of God, you take away
    the sins of the world   have mercy on us
Lamb of God, you take away
    the sins of the world   have mercy on us
Lamb of God, you take away
    the sins of the world   have mercy on us

V. God made him master of his household.
R. And put him in charge of all that he owned.

Let us pray.

Almighty God,
in your infinite wisdom and love
you chose Joseph to be the husband of Mary,
the mother of your Son.
As we enjoy his protection on earth
may we have the help of his prayers in heaven.
We ask this through Christ our Lord.

Amen.

Novena in Honor of the Immaculate Conception of the Blessed Virgin Mary

114. The custom of praying for nine successive days prior to the celebration of a major solemnity or feast is suggested by the nine days the apostles spent in Jerusalem at the Lord's command as they awaited the coming of the Holy Spirit (see Luke 24:49; Acts 1:4).

The devotional novena first appeared in the Middle Ages in France and Spain as a preparatory period prior to the celebration of Christmas, the number nine (9) representing the nine months Jesus spent in the womb of the Virgin Mary. The "O antiphons" of Advent of the Liturgy of the Hours (December 17-24) are a liturgical vestige of the early Advent novena. Novenas to prepare for the feasts of Mary or one of the saints grew out of that custom. It was not until the nineteenth century that the Church recommended the practice.

The following novena is especially appropriate for the nine days that precede the solemnity of the Immaculate Conception of the Blessed Virgin Mary, December 8. It may be celebrated in public or in private.

NOVENA IN HONOR OF THE IMMACULATE CONCEPTION OF THE BLESSED VIRGIN MARY

Leader:

Let us pray.

Pause for silent prayer.

Almighty Father,
we offer this novena to honor the Blessed Virgin Mary.
She occupies a place in the Church which is highest after Christ
and yet very close to us
for you chose her to give the world
that very Life which renews all things,
Jesus Christ, your Son and our Lord.

And so we praise you, Mary, virgin and mother.
After the Savior himself, you alone are all holy,
free from the stain of sin,
gifted by God from the first instant of your conception
with a unique holiness.

R. We praise and honor you.

Mary, free from all sin and led by the Holy Spirit,
you embraced God's saving will with a full heart,
and devoted yourself totally as a handmaid of the Lord
to the fulfillment of his will in your life,
and to the mystery of our redemption.

R. We thank you and love you.

Mary, your privileged and grace-filled origin
is the Father's final step in preparing humanity
to receive its Redeemer in human form.
Your fullness of grace is the Father's sign of his favor to the Church
and also his promise to the Church
of its perfection as the Bride of Christ,
radiant in beauty.

Your holiness in the beginning of your life
is the foreshadowing of that all-embracing holiness
with which the Father will surround his people
when his Son comes at the end of time to greet us.

R. We bless you among all women.

All:

Mary, we turn with confidence to you,
who are always ready to listen with a mother's affection
and powerful assistance.
Consoler of the afflicted,
Health of the sick,
Refuge of sinners,
grant us comfort in tribulation,
relief in sickness,
and liberating strength in our weakness.

You who are free from sin, lead us to combat sin.
Obtain for us the victory of hope over anguish,
of joy and beauty over boredom and disgust,
of eternal visions over temporal ones,
of life over death.
Mary, conceived without sin,
pray for us who have recourse to you.

(Individual petitions are mentioned here)

81

Leader:

Let us pray.

Pause for silent prayer.

God our Father,
we make these petitions through Mary.
We pray most especially for the coming of your kingdom.
May you, together with your Son and the Holy Spirit,
be known, loved and glorified
and your law of love faithfully followed.
We pray in faith through Jesus Christ, your Son and our Lord,
in whom all fullness dwells,
now and for ever.

R. Amen.

Biblical Readings

115. The texts of the following biblical readings are given in the Lectionary for Mass, Common of the Blessed Virgin Mary, nos. 707-712.

Reading I: Outside the Easter Season (no. 707)

Genesis 3:9-15,20 I will put enmity between your offspring and her offspring.
Genesis 12:1-7 He spoke to our fathers, to Abraham and his seed forever.
2 Samuel 7:1-5,8-11,16 God will give him the seat of David, his father.
1 Chronicles 15:3-4,15-16;16:1-2 They brought the ark of God in and put it inside the tent that David had pitched for it.
Proverbs 8:22-31 Mary, seat of wisdom.
Sirach 24:1,3-4,8-12,19-21 Mary, seat of wisdom.
Isaiah 7:10-14 Behold, the virgin shall conceive.
Isaiah 9:1-6 A Son is born to us.
Isaiah 61:9-11 I will rejoice in my God.
Micah 5:1-4 The remnant will return when she who is pregnant gives birth.
Zechariah 2:14-17 Rejoice, daughter of Zion, for I am coming.

Reading I: During the Easter Season (no. 708)

Acts 1:12-14 They all joined in continuous prayer together with Jesus' mother, Mary.
Revelation 11:19;12:1-6,10 A great sign appeared in the heavens.
Revelation 21:1-5 I saw the new Jerusalem, as beautiful as a bride all dressed for her husband.

Responsorial Psalm (709)

1 Samuel 2:1,4-5,6-7,8
R. My heart rejoices in the Lord, my Savior.

Judith 13:18,19,20
R. You are the highest honor of our race.

Psalm 45:11-12,14-15,16-17
R. Listen to me, daughter; see and bend your ear.

Psalm 113:1-2,3-4,5-6,7-8
R. Blessed be the name of the Lord for ever.

Luke 1:46-47,48-49,50-51,52-53,54-55
R. The Almighty has done great things for me and holy is his name.

Reading II (no. 710)

Romans 5:12,17-19 However great the number of sins committed, grace was even greater.
Romans 8:28-30 God knew them and called them to justification.
Galatian 4:4-7 God sent his Son, born of a woman.
Ephesians 1:3-6,11-12 Before the world was made, God chose us in Christ.

Gospel (no. 712)

Matthew 1:1-16,18-23 (Long Form)
Matthew 1:18-23 (Short Form) She has conceived and what is in her is by the Holy Spirit.
Matthew 2:13-15,19-23 Take the child and his mother and flee into Egypt.
Luke 1:26-38 You will conceive and bear a son.
Luke 1:39-47 Blessed is she who believed.
Luke 2:1-14 She gave birth to a son, her firstborn.
Luke 2:15-19 Mary treasured all these things and pondered them in her heart.
Luke 2:27-35 A sword will pierce your own soul.
Luke 2:41-52 Your father and I have been looking for you.
Luke 11:27-28 Happy the womb that bore you!
John 2:1-11 The mother of Jesus was at the wedding feast with him.
John 19:25-27 Woman, this is your son. This is your mother.

Non-Biblical Readings

116. The following non-biblical readings may be used in any of the Marian services, either in place of the homily or as an additional reading.

A. *Homily of Saint Bede the Venerable, priest*, Lib. 1,4: CCL 122,25-26.30,
"Mary Proclaims the Greatness of the Lord Working in Her"

A reading from a *Homily of Saint Bede the Venerable.*

My soul proclaims the greatness of the Lord, and my spirit rejoices in God my savior. With these words Mary first acknowledges the special gifts she has been given. Then she recalls God's universal favors, bestowed unceasingly on the human race.

When a man devotes all his thoughts to the praise and service of the Lord, he proclaims God's greatness. His observance of God's commands, moreover, shows that he has God's power and greatness always at heart. His spirit rejoices in God his savior and delights in the mere recollection of his creator who gives him hope for eternal salvation.

These words are often for all God's creations, but especially for the Mother of God. She alone was chosen, and she burned with spiritual love for the son she so joyously conceived. Above all other saints, she alone could truly rejoice in Jesus, her savior, for she knew that he who was the source of eternal salvation would be born in time in her body, in one person both her own son and her Lord.

For the Almighty has done great things for me, and holy is his name. Mary attributes nothing to her own merits. She refers all her greatness to the gift of the one whose essence is power and whose nature is greatness, for he fills with greatness and strength the small and the weak who believe in him.

She did well to add: and holy is his name, to warn those who heard, and indeed all who would receive his words, that they must believe and call upon his name. For they too could share in everlasting holiness and true salvation according to the words of the prophet: and it will come to pass, that everyone who calls on the name of the Lord will be saved. This is the name she spoke of earlier: and my spirit rejoices in God my savior.

Therefore, it is an excellent and fruitful custom of holy Church that we should sing Mary's hymn at the time of evening prayer. By meditating upon the incarnation, our devotion is kindled, and by remembering the example of God's Mother, we are encouraged to lead a life of virtue. Such virtues are best achieved in the evening. We are weary after the day's work and worn out by our distractions. The time for rest is near, and our minds are ready for contemplation.

B. *Lumen Gentium* (*Dogmatic Constitution on the Church*), ch. 2, no. 55, "The Role of the Blessed Virgin in the Economy of Salvation"

A reading from the *Dogmatic Constitution on the Church* of the Second Vatican Council.

The sacred Scriptures of both the Old and New Testament, as well as ancient tradition, show the role of the Mother of the Savior in the economy of salvation in an ever clearer light and propose it as something to be probed into. The books of the Old Testament recount the period of salvation history during which the coming of Christ into the world was slowly prepared for. These earliest documents, as they are read in the Church, and are understood in the light of a further and full revelation, bring the figure of the woman, Mother of the Redeemer, into a gradually sharper focus.

When looked at in this way, she is already prophetically foreshadowed in that victory over the serpent which was promised to our first parents after their fall into sin (Gn 3:15). Likewise she is the Virgin who is to conceive and bear a son, whose name will be called Emmanuel (cf. Is 7:14; Mi 5:2-3; Mt 1:22-23). She stands out among the poor and humble of the Lord, who confidently await and receive salvation from Him. With her, the exalted Daughter of Sion [Zion], and after long expectation of the promise, the times were at length fulfilled and the new dispensation established. All this occurred when the Son of God took a human nature from her, that He might in the mysteries of his flesh free man from sin.

C. *Lumen Gentium* (*Dogmatic Constitution on the Church*), ch. 3, no. 61, "The Blessed Virgin and the Church"

A reading from the *Dogmatic Constitution on the Church* of the Second Vatican Council.

The Blessed Virgin was eternally predestined, in conjunction with the incarnation of the divine Word, to be the Mother of God. By decree of divine Providence, she served on earth as the loving mother of the divine Redeemer, an associate of unique nobility, and the Lord's humble handmaid. She conceived, brought forth, and nourished Christ. She presented Him to the Father in the temple and was united with Him in suffering as He died on the cross. In an utterly singular way she cooperated by her obedience, faith, hope, and burning charity in the Savior's work of restoring supernatural life to our souls. For this reason she is a mother to us in the order of grace.

D. Apostolic Exhortation *Marialis cultus*, Pope Paul VI (February 2, 1974), no. 17, "Mary Is the Attentive Virgin"

A reading from the Apostolic Exhortation of Pope Paul VI on Marian Worship.

Mary is the *attentive Virgin*, who receives the word of God with faith, that faith which in her case was the gateway and path to divine Motherhood, for, as Saint Augustine realized,

"Blessed Mary by believing conceived him (Jesus) whom believing she brought forth." In fact, when she received from the angel the answer to her doubt (cf. Lk 1:34-37), "full of faith and conceiving Christ in her mind before conceiving him in her womb, she said, 'I am the handmaid of the Lord, let what you have said be done to me' (Lk 1:38)." It was faith that was for her the cause of blessedness and certainty in the fulfillment of the promise: "Blessed is she who believed that the promise made her by the Lord would be fulfilled" (Lk 1:45). Similarly, it was faith with which she, who played a part in the Incarnation and was a unique witness to it, thinking back on the events of the infancy of Christ, meditated upon these events in her heart (cf. Lk 2:19,51). The Church also acts in this way, especially in the liturgy, when with faith she listens, accepts, proclaims and venerates the word of God, distributes it to the faithful as the bread of life and in the light of that word examines the signs of the times and interprets and lives the events of history.

E.   Apostolic Exhortation *Marialis cultus*, Pope Paul VI (February 2, 1974), no. 21,
"Mary, Teacher of the Spiritual Life"

A reading from the Apostolic Exhortation of Pope Paul VI on Marian Worship.

Mary is not only an example for the whole Church in the exercise of divine worship but is also, clearly, a teacher of the spiritual life for individual Christians. The faithful at a very early date began to look to Mary and to imitate her in making their lives an act of worship of God and making their worship a commitment of their lives. As early as the fourth century, Saint Ambrose, speaking to the people, expressed the hope that each of them would have the spirit of Mary in order to glorify God: "May the heart of Mary be in each Christian to proclaim the greatness of the Lord; may her spirit be in everyone to exult in God." But Mary is above all the example of that worship that consists in making one's life an offering to God. This is an ancient and ever new doctrine that each individual can hear again by heeding the Church's teaching, but also by heeding the very voice of the Virgin as she, anticipating in herself the wonderful petition of the Lord's Prayer—"Your will be done" (Mt 6:10)—replied to God's messenger: "I am the handmaid of the Lord. Let what you have said be done to me" (Lk 1:38). And Mary's "yes" is for all Christians a lesson and example of obedience to the will of the Father, which is the way and means of one's own sanctification.

F.   Encyclical Letter *Redemptor Hominis*, Pope John Paul II (March 4, 1979), no. 22,
"The Mother in Whom We Trust"

A reading from the Encyclical Letter *Redemptor Hominis* of Pope John Paul II.

. . . [T]he Church always, and particularly at our time, has need of a Mother. . . . Mary is Mother of the Church because, on account of the Eternal Father's ineffable choice and due to the Spirit of Love's special action, she gave human life to the Son of God "for whom and by whom all things exist" and from whom the whole People of God receives the grace and dignity of election. Her Son explicitly extended his Mother's maternity in a way that could easily be understood by every soul and every heart by designating, when he was raised on the Cross, his beloved disciple as her son. The Holy Spirit inspired her to remain in the Upper Room, after our Lord's Ascension, recollected in prayer and expectation, together with the Apostles, until the day of Pentecost, when the Church was born in visible form, coming forth from darkness. Later, all the generations of disciples of those who confess and love Christ, like the Apostle John, spiritually took this Mother to their own homes, and she was thus included in the history of salvation and in the Church's mission from the very beginning, that is from the moment of the Annunciation. Accordingly, we who form today's generation of disciples of Christ all wish to unite ourselves with her in a special way. . . .

G. Encyclical Letter *Redemptor Hominis*, Pope John Paul II, March 4, 1979, no. 22, "The Mother in Whom We Trust"

A reading from the Encyclical Letter *Redemptor Hominis* of Pope John Paul II.

. . . [I]f we feel a special need, in this difficult and responsible phase of the history of the Church and of mankind, to turn to Christ, who is Lord of the Church and Lord of man's history on account of the mystery of the Redemption, we believe that nobody else can bring us as Mary can into the divine and human dimension of his mystery. Nobody has been brought into it by God himself as Mary has. It is in this that the exceptional character of the grace of the divine Motherhood consists. . . .

We can say that the mystery of Redemption took shape beneath the heart of the Virgin of Nazareth when she pronounced her "fiat." From then on, under the special influence of the Holy Spirit, this heart, the heart of both a virgin and a mother, has always followed the work of her Son and has gone out to all those whom Christ has embraced and continues to embrace with inexhaustible love. . . .

H. Encyclical Letter, *Redemptoris Mater*, Pope John Paul II, March 25, 1987, no. 36 "In the Magnificat Mary Proclaims Her Faith"

A reading from the Encyclical Letter *Redemptoris Mater* of Pope John Paul II.

When Elizabeth greeted her young kinswoman coming from Nazareth, *Mary replied with the Magnificat.* In her greeting, Elizabeth first called Mary "blessed" because of "the fruit of her womb," and then she called her "blessed" because of her faith (cf. Lk 1:42,45). These two blessings referred directly to the Annunciation. Now, at the Visitation, when Elizabeth's greeting bears witness to that culminating moment, Mary's faith acquires a new consciousness and a new expression. That which remained hidden in the depths of the "obedience of faith" at the Annunciation can now be said to spring forth like a clear and life-giving flame of the spirit. The words used by Mary on the threshold of Elizabeth's house are *an inspired profession of her faith,* in which *her response to the revealed word* is expressed with the religious and poetical exultation of her whole being towards God. In these sublime words, which are simultaneously very simple and wholly inspired by the sacred texts of the people of Israel, Mary's personal experience, the ecstasy of her heart, shines forth. In them shines a ray of the mystery of God, the glory of his ineffable holiness, the eternal *love which, as an irrevocable gift, enters into human history.*

Mary is the first to share in this new revelation of God and, within the same, in this new "self-giving" of God. Therefore she proclaims: "For he who is mighty has done great things for me, and holy is his name." Her words reflect a joy of spirit which is difficult to express: "My spirit rejoices in God my Savior." Indeed, "the deepest truth about God and the salvation of man is made clear to us in Christ, who is at the same time the mediator and the fullness of all revelation." In her exultation Mary confesses that she finds herself *in the very heart of this fullness* of Christ. She is conscious that the promise made to the fathers, first of all "to Abraham and to his posterity for ever," is being fulfilled in herself. She is thus aware that concentrated within herself as the Mother of Christ is *the whole salvific economy,* in which "from age to age" is manifested he who, as the God of the Covenant, "remembers his mercy."

I.   Encyclical Letter, *Redemptoris Mater,* Pope John Paul II, March 25, 1987, no. 37
"The Magnificat of the Pilgrim Church"

A reading from the Encyclical Letter *Redemptoris Mater* of Pope John Paul II.

The Church, which from the beginning has modelled her earthly journey on that of the Mother of God, constantly repeats after her the words of the *Magnificat.* From the depths of the Virgin's faith at the Annunciation and the Visitation, the Church derives the truth about the God of the Covenant: the God who is Almighty and does "great things" for man: "holy is his name." In the *Magnificat* the Church sees uprooted that sin which is found at the outset of the earthly history of man and woman, the sin of disbelief and of "little faith" in God. In contrast with the "suspicion" which the "father of lies" sowed in the heart of Eve the first woman, Mary, whom tradition is wont to call the "new Eve" and the true "Mother of the living," boldly proclaims the *undimmed* truth about God: the holy and almighty God, who from the beginning is *the source of all gifts,* he who "has done great things" in her, as well as in the whole universe. In the act of creation God gives existence to all that is. In creating man, God gives him the dignity of the image and likeness of himself in a special way as compared with all earthly creatures. Moreover, in his desire to give, *God gives himself in the Son,* notwithstanding man's sin: "He so loved the world that he gave his only Son" (Jn 3:16). Mary is the first witness of this marvellous truth, which will be fully accomplished through "the works and words" (cf. Acts 1:1) of her Son and definitively through his Cross and Resurrection.

The Church, which even "amid trials and tribulations" does not cease repeating with Mary the words of the *Magnificat,* is sustained by the power of God's truth, proclaimed on that occasion with such extraordinary simplicity. At the same time, *by means of this truth about God* the Church *desires to shed light upon* the difficult and sometimes tangled paths of man's earthly existence. The Church's journey, therefore, near the end of the second Christian Millennium, involves a renewed commitment to her mission. Following him who said of himself: "(God) has anointed me *to preach good news to the poor*" (cf. Lk 4:18), the Church has sought from generation to generation and still seeks today to accomplish that same mission.

The Church's *love of preference for the poor* is wonderfully inscribed in Mary's *Magnificat.* The God of the Covenant, celebrated in the exultation of her spirit by the Virgin of Nazareth, is also he who "has cast down the mighty from their thrones, and lifted up the lowly, . . . filled the hungry with good things, sent the rich away empty, . . . scattered the proud-hearted . . . and his mercy is from age to age on those who fear him." Mary is deeply imbued with the spirit of the "poor of Yahweh," who in the prayer of the Psalms awaited from God their salvation, placing all their trust in him (cf. Pss 25;31;35; 55). Mary truly proclaims the coming of the "Messiah of the poor" (cf. Is 11:4;61:1). Drawing from Mary's heart, from the depth of her faith expressed in the words of the *Magnificat*, the Church renews ever more effectively in herself the awareness that *the truth about God who saves*, the truth about God who is the source of every gift, *cannot be separated from the manifestation of his love of preference for the poor and humble*, that love which, celebrated in the *Magnificat*, is later expressed in the words and works of Jesus.

The Church is thus aware—and at the present time this awareness is particularly vivid—not only that these two elements of the message contained in the *Magnificat* cannot be separated, but also that there is a duty to safeguard carefully the importance of "the poor" and of "the option in favor of the poor" in the word of the living God. These matters and questions are intimately connected with the *Christian meaning of freedom and liberation.* "Mary is totally dependent upon God and completely directed towards him, and, at the side of her Son, she is the most perfect image of freedom and of the liberation of humanity and of the universe. It is to her as Mother and Model that the Church must look in order to understand in its completeness the meaning of her own mission."

J. Pastoral Letter *Behold Your Mother: Woman of Faith*, National Conference of Catholic Bishops (November 21, 1973), no. 71, "Our Blessed Mother"

A reading from the Pastoral Letter of the National Conference of Catholic Bishops, *Behold Your Mother: Woman of Faith*, no. 71.

It is important to understand what is meant by the title, "our Blessed Mother." Mary is not spiritual mother of men solely because she was physical Mother of the Savior. Nonetheless, the full understanding of Mary's motherhood of Jesus contains also the secret of her spiritual motherhood of the brethren of Christ. This secret is the truth already given in the Gospels and constantly stressed ever since in Christian thought and piety: Mary consented *in faith* to become the Mother of Jesus. The Second Vatican Council was in the stream of the constant tradition of the Church when it said that Mary received the Word of God into her heart and her body at the angel's announcement and thereby brought life to the world. She conceived in her heart, with her whole being, before she conceived in her womb. First came Mary's faith, then her motherhood. Faith is the key also to the spiritual motherhood of Mary. By her faith she became the perfect example of what the Gospels mean by "spiritual motherhood." In the preaching of the Savior, His "mother" is whoever hears God's word and keeps it. All who truly follow Christ become "mothers" of Christ, for by their faith they bring Him to birth in others.

K. Pastoral Letter *Behold Your Mother: Woman of Faith*, National Conference of Catholic Bishops (November 21, 1973), nos. 81-82, "Mary in Our Life"

A reading from the Pastoral Letter of the National Conference of Catholic Bishops, *Behold Your Mother: Woman of Faith*, nos. 81-82.

According to the *Constitution on the Sacred Liturgy*, the Church honors the Mother of God when it celebrates the cycle of Christ's saving mysteries. For "Blessed Mary is joined by an inseparable bond to the saving work of her Son." Deeper Biblical insights have increased our awareness of Mary as the model of faithful discipleship; but it is also our purpose here to reinforce our Catholic sense of the Blessed Mother's present concern for us in her union with the risen Christ.

Since early times, but especially after the Council of Ephesus, devotion to Mary in the Church has grown wondrously. The People of God through the ages have shown her veneration and love. They have called upon her in prayer and they imitate her. All these ways of praising Mary draw us closer to Christ. When Mary is honored, her Son is duly acknowledged, loved and glorified, and His commandments are observed. To venerate Mary correctly means to acknowledge her Son, for she is the Mother of God. To love her means to love Jesus, for she is always the Mother of Jesus. To pray to our Lady means not to substitute her for Christ, but to glorify her Son who desires us to have loving confidence in His Saints, especially in His Mother. To imitate the "faithful Virgin" means to keep her Son's commandments.

Musical Resources

117. The following is a list of Marian hymns, choral anthems, and organ music, which are appropriate for use in any of the services.

Hymnals

Glory and Praise: Parish Music Program
Phoenix, Arizona: North American Liturgy Resources, 1984.
—Dwelling Place
—Earthen Vessels (especially stanza 2)
—Hail Mary, Gentle Woman
—Hail, Holy Queen
—I Have Loved You
—My Soul Rejoices
—Only a Shadow
—Service
—Sing a New Song
—Take, Lord, Receive

ICEL Resource Collection of Hymns and Service Music for the Liturgy
Chicago, Illinois: G.I.A. Publications, 1981.
—Ave Maria (Chant)
—Be Joyful, Mary, Heav'nly Queen
—Canticle of Mary
—Hail! Holy Queen Enthroned Above
—Hail, Queen of Heav'n
—Immaculate Mary
—Magnificat (Psalm Tone)
—O Purest of Creatures!
—Praise We the Lord This Day
—Salve, Regina
—The God Whom Earth and Sea and Sky
—Who Is She Ascends So High

Worship: A Hymnal and Service Book for Roman Catholics
Chicago, Illinois: G.I.A. Publications, 1986 (Third Edition).
—At the Cross Her Station Keeping (Lent)
—Ave Maria (Chant)
—Be Joyful, Mary (Easter)
—Hail, Holy Queen Enthroned Above
—Hail, Queen of Heaven/Salve, Regina (Chant)
—Immaculate Mary
—Let Us with Joy Our Voices Raise
—Lo, How a Rose E'er Blooming (Christmas)
—Magnificat (Canon)
—Mary, How Lovely the Light of Your Glory
—O Queen of Heaven/Regina Caeli (Chant-Easter)
—O Sanctissima
—Sing We of the Blessed Mother
—Sing of Mary, Pure and Lowly
—Tell Out, My Soul, the Greatness of the Lord
—The Angel Gabriel from Heaven Came (Annunciation)
—The God Whom Earth and Sea and Sky
—Virgin-born, We Bow before You

Peoples Mass Book
Schiller Park, Illinois: World Library Publications, 1984.
—Canticle of Mary
—Canticle of Our Lady (Psalm Tone)
—Hail, Blessed Lady/Salve, Regina
—Hail, Holy Queen Enthroned Above
—Hail, Queen of Heaven
—Holy Mary, Now We Crown You
—Mary the Dawn
—O Mary, of All Women
—She Will Show Us the Promised One
—Sing of Mary
—Sing to Mary, Mother Most Merciful
—Star upon the Ocean
—Virgin, Full of Grace

1987 Assembly Book, Cycle A
Phoenix/Toronto/Cincinnati: North American Liturgy Resources, 1986.
—All the Ends of the Earth
—By Name I Have Called You
—Faithful Love
—Gospel Canticle
—Hail Mary, Gentle Woman
—Here I Am, Lord
—Immaculate Mary
—Mary's Song
—My Soul Rejoices

—O Chosen One
—Pieta
—Praised Be the Flower
—Spirit of God

Today's Missal—Music Issue 1987
Portland, Oregon: Oregon Catholic Press, 1987.
—Magnificat
—Mary's Song
—Mary, Full of Grace
—O God, Hear Us
—O Queen of Heaven
—Sing of Mary
—Star above the Ocean

We Celebrate
Chicago, Illinois: J. S. Paluch Company, Inc., 1982.
—Ave Maria/Hail, Maiden Mary
—Canticle of Mary
—Daily, Daily Sing to Mary
—Hail, Holy Queen Enthroned Above
—Holy Mary, Now We Crown You
—Immaculate Mary
—Memorare
—O Most Holy One
—O Queen of Heaven
—O Sanctissima
—Our Lady's Song of Praise
—Salve, Regina Coelitum
—She Will Show Us the Promised One
—Sing of Mary
—Stainless the Maiden
—Virgin, Full of Grace

Canticos de Gracias y Alabanza
Portland, Oregon: Oregon Catholic Press, 1982.
—Adiós, Reina del Cielo
—Ave María
—Humilde Nazarena
—Madre Dolorosa
—Madre de Todos los Hombres
—Madre de los Pobres
—Madre del Amor
—Oh Virgen de Guadalupe
—Oh Virgen sin Mancha
—Oh Santísima
—Viva la Virgen de Guadalupe

Cantemos al Senor
Miami, Florida: Archdiocese of Miami, 1986.
—Ave María
—Ave María, Caridad de Cobre
—Cancíon de María
—Canto de María
—Dios Te Salve María
—La Virgen Sueña Caminos
—Madre de Nuestra Alegría
—Madre de la Iglesia
—Madre de los Jovenes
—Magnificat
—Oh María
—Oh Santísima
—Saludo a María
—Salve, Regina (Chant)
—Santa María del Camino
—Virgen Mambisa
—Virgencita del Cobre

Evening Prayer for Feasts of Mary
    For a complete musical setting of Evening Prayer for solemnities and feasts of the Blessed Virgin Mary, see *Evening Prayer for Feasts of Mary* (minister's and people's editions). Washington, D.C.: Federation of Diocesan Liturgical Commissions, 1979.

Plainsong

Alma Redemptoris Mater	Regina Coeli, Jubila
Ave Maria	Regina Coeli, Laetare
Ave, Regina Coelorum	Salve, Mater Misericordiae
Magnificat	Salve, Regina

Choral Music

Alma Redemptoris Mater	Any setting; plainsong; Anerio, Palestrina, Mozart
Assumpta Est Maria	Many settings; Palestrina, Aichinger, Prenner
Ave Maria Virgo Serena	Josquin
Ave Maria	Any setting; plainsong; Palestrina, Victoria, Mouton, Alain, Poulenc, Clemens non Papa, Senil, Arcadelt, Stravinsky
Ave Maris Stella	Any setting; plainsong; Hassler
Conceptio Tua	Marenzio

Hodie Maria Virgo Ascendit	Erbach
Litanies a la vièrge noire	Poulenc
Magnificat	Any setting; plainsong; Latin and English settings by many composers
Marienlieder	Brahms
Salve, Regina	Any setting; plainsong; Poulenc, Désenclos, Guerrero
Tota Pulchra Es	Durufle, Campra, Schuetz, Monteverdi

Organ Music

Annonciation	Dupré
Ave Maria	Reger, Langlais (Ave Maria, Ave Maris Stella)
Ave maris stella	Settings by Cabézon, Frescobaldi, Coelho, de Grigny, Dandrieu, Franck, Dupré, Tournemire (Improvisation), Peeters (Toccata, Fugue et Hymne), Tippett (Prelude to the Vespers of Monteverdi)
Canto Llano de la Inmaculada Concepcion	Correa de Arauxo (variations)
L'Angelus	Dupré
L'Orgue Mystique	Tournemire (Nos. 2, 11, 35, and 42)
Magnificat	Verses for organ by Cabezón, Frescobaldi, Scheidt, Scheidemann, Kindermann, Lebègue, Guilain, Dandrieu, M. Corrette, Guilmant, Dupré; Preludes and individual settings by Buxtehude, Pachelbel, Bach (Fuge; Schubler Chorale)
Maria zu lieben	Hurford (Five verses on a melody from the Paderborn Gesangbuch)
Regina Coeli	Schroeder (Marianischen Antiphone)
Salve, Regina	Settings by Cabezón, Caurroy, Cornet, Widor (Symphony 2), Dupré (Choral et Fuge)
Suite Mariale	Maleingreau

Collections   *Notre Dame; A la Vièrge* (Orgue et Liturgie
                                             Nos. 11 and 14)
                            A la Sainte Vièrge; Salve, Regina (L'Organiste
                                             Liturgique Nos. 2 and 21)
                            Marienleste (Cantantibus Organis, No. 19)